EUROPE
speaks
ARABIC

DR V. ABDUR RAHIM

لقـًا

Institute of the Language of the Quran, Toronto, Canada
www.lqtoronto.com

GOODWORD
www.goodwordbooks.com

First published 2008
Reprinted 2009
© V Abdur Rahim 2008

Published by

Institute of the Language of the Quran Inc.
3077 Weston Road, Suite 1912
Toronto ON Canada M9M 3A1
Te' and Fax # 416-496-6103
email: lugatulquran@hotmail.com
www.lgtoronto.com

Distributed by

Goodword Books
1, Nizamuddin West Market
New Delhi - 110 013
Tel. +9111 2435 5454, 2435 6666
Fax: +9111 2435 7333
email: info@goodwordbooks.com
www.goodwordbooks.com

Printed in India

CONTENTS

PREFACE

Arabic gave Europe cotton to wear, candy to eat, coffee to drink, chess to play, magazine to read, sofa to recline on, mattress to sleep on, cipher to calculate with, cable to communicate with, racket to play tennis with, sugar to sweeten with, cheque to draw money with, and a host of other words.

This book intends to tell the common reader about these words in simple non-technical language with a view to creating in them an interest in, and understanding of, our common cultural heritage. As the reader will discover, in many cases Arabic provided the name and the raw material, and Europe developed it into a highly sophisticated finished product like *lubān jāwī* which was turned into *benzene*!

Arabic provided Europe with the Arabic numerals to replace the cumbersome Roman numerals which would not have created even the crudest form of calculator. This new system of calculation laid the foundation of modern science and technology. The adoption of this system has left its traces on the language. The Arabic *ṣifr* literally meaning empty, and used to represent zero, became *cipher* in English, and as the most important element in the new system, came to mean the whole system of Arabic enumeration. As the use of this mode of calculation was at first confined to scientists, and the *hoi polloi* had no knowledge of it, the word came to mean a secret language or a code. And to *decipher* came to mean to decode. It is interesting to note that the French form of the word *chiffre* has returned to modern Arabic in the form of *šifrah* (شِفْرَة) meaning a code, and words like *tašfīr* (coding), and *mušaffar* (coded) have been derived from it.

Who would believe that the word *exchequer* meaning the British department of revenue can be of Arabic origin? Yet, that is the linguistic fact. It was so named from the chequered cloth covering the table on which the accounts were reckoned! *Chequer* (also *checker*) formerly meant a chessboard. And a *chequered* cloth is one with designs as on the chessboard. *Check* ultimately comes from the Persian word *šāh* used in Arabic for the king in chess, and means a warning given by chess players to their adversaries to guard their king. Later it came to mean to bring something to a standstill, to restrain, to hinder, to control, to verify. In this last sense it was later applied to the counterfoil of a bank bill as it is a means to check forgery. When it became a powerful instrument of monetary transaction, the British gave it a dignified look by changing its spelling from *check* to *cheque* (though the Americans did not go in for this plastic surgery). The Arabs after centuries imported their own *šāh* after he had been transformed into a useful piece of paper now called *šēk*.

In modern Arabic, a spark-plug is *būjī* (بوجي) which is from the French *bougie d'allumage*. Only the linguists among the French and the Arabs know that the French *bougie* meaning candle-wax is a corruption of *Bijāyaħ*, the name of a city in Algiers which exported wax.

Arab seafaring has left its trace on European languages. The Arabic *ʿawāriyyaħ* meaning goods damaged during sea transport became *averia* in Spanish meaning damage sustained by merchandise during transport. In Italian, *avaria* means damage at sea, and in Portuguese just damage without reference to the sea. The French *avarie*, though formerly meaning damage to merchandise during sea transport, now includes land and air transport as well. By adding -*age* to the French form of the word, English created *average* which formerly meant expense or loss by damage of ship or cargo. Then it came to mean the equitable distribution of such loss among the parties concerned. And from this last meaning developed the sense of arithmetical mean which is not found in other languages.

I earnestly hope that this book will accredit the Arabic words embedded in European languages to be goodwill ambassadors of Arabic, and to contribute, in no small measure, to a sympathetic understanding of its useful role in human history.

Al-Madīnaḥ,   V. Abdur Rahim
Rabīʿ al-Awwal 12, 1429 AH
March 23, 2008 CE[1]

---

1 As *AD* stands for *Anno Domini* meaning 'In the year of (our) Lord', some non-Christians prefer to use *CE* meaning *Common* or *Christian Era*.

INTRODUCTION

This book discusses Arabic words used in English and some other European languages. Only selected words have been discussed in this work.

Among the Romance languages, I regularly mention French, Spanish, Portuguese and Italian. I occasionally mention Provençal and Rumanian, the former when its form has a special feature, and the latter mostly in the context of Arabic words that have passed into the Balkan languages through Turkish.

Among the Germanic languages, I regularly mention German, Dutch, Danish and Swedish, and among the Slavic languages, Russian and Macedonian, and occasionally Serbo-Croatian and Polish.

Some languages like modern Greek, Albanian and Esperanto are occasionally mentioned.

I occasionally mention the form of the word in medieval Latin if it helps us understand the Romance form of the Arabic word.

Only words recognized by European linguists as borrowings from Arabic, and mentioned in reputed dictionaries, are included in this book.

* * * * *

DICTIONARIES CONSULTED

English:
1) *The Oxford English Dictionary* (OED).
2) *The New Shorter Oxford English Dictionary* (NSOED).
3) *Oxford Concise Dictionary of English Etymology* by T. F. Hoad (OCDEE).
4) *Webster's New Universal Unabridged Dictionary* (WNUUD).
5) *Chambers's Twentieth Century Dictionary* (CTCD).
6) *Oxford Advanced Learner's Dictionary* (OALD). I have mostly followed this dictionary with regard to modern usage, spelling, etc.

Other languages:
  1) *Glossaire des mots espagnols et portugais
     dérivés de l'arabe* by Reinhart Dozy & Dr
     W. H. Engelman.
  2) *Le Petit Robert.*
  3) *Etymologisches Wörterbuch der europäi-
     schen Wörter orientalischen Ursprungs* by
     Karl Lokotsch.
  4) *Fremdwörter Lexikon* by Gerhard Wahrig.

*****

THE ARABIC ALPHABET
Pronunciation and Phonetic Notation

(a) The Consonants
The following are the letters of the Arabic
alphabet with their corresponding letters and
signs used in this book:

ء ٔ   It is the glottal stop which is like the
       Cockney pronunciation of *tt* in *butter,
       bottle, rotten,* etc. In this book, the sign
       of *hamzah* is not indicated at the begin-
       ning of a word. A word commencing
       with a vowel in fact commences with a
       hamzah, e.g. *amīr* (*'amīr*).
ب b   as *b* in *book.*

ت	t	as *t* in *cat* but softer.
ث	th	as *th* in *think*.
ج	j	as *j* in *just*.
ح	ḥ	A voiceless guttural fricative. Its voiced counterpart is ع. It is as *h* in *hand*, but stronger.
خ	kh	similar to *ch* in the Scotch *loch*, or the German *Buch*, but unlike the European sound, it is guttural not velar.
د	d	as *d* in *do*, but softer.
ذ	dh	as *th* in *that*.
ر	r	as *r* in *run*.
ز	z	as *z* in *zoo*.
س	s	as *s* in *sun*, never as in *rose*.
ش	š	as *sh* is *she*.
ص	ṣ	a velarized form of *s*.
ض	ḍ	a velarized interdental fricative. It is somewhat like *th* in *this*.
ط	ṭ	a velarized form of *t*.
ظ	ẓ	a velarized form of ذ (*dh*).
ع	ʿ	a voiced guttural fricative. See ح. It has no approximate equivalent in English. It may be ignored at the beginning of a word as in ʿawār, and when it occurs after a vowel as in taʿrīf, the vowel may be lengthened.

غ   gh   a voiced form of خ. *G* as in *good* may be substituted for it.

ف   f   as *f* in *food*.

ق   q   a voiceless uvular stop. It is a strongly articulated *k.*

ك   k   as *k* in *book*.

ل   l   as *l* in *love*. But in the word *Allah*, it is velarized.

م   m   as *m* in *moon*.

ن   n   as *n* in *noon*.

و   w   as *w* in *wall*.

ه   h   as *h* in *hand*.

ي   y   as *y* in *you*.

ة   ħ   called *the round tā*, it occurs only at the end of a word. It is pronounced *t,* but changes to *h* in the pausal form.[1]

(b) The Vowels

The three short vowels of Arabic are:

fatḥaħ: as *a* in *bat.*

---

[1] The pausal form of a word is the one it assumes when it happens to be the last word in a sentence, e.g. *hādhihī makkatu, wa ana uḥubbu makkah* (This is Makkaħ and I love Makkaħ). Note that in the non-pausal form, it is *makkat-u* and in the pausal form *makkah*. The letter ة is basically ه to which the two dots of ت have been added to point to its dual pronunciation. The roman character I use to represent this letter (ħ) also combines *h* and *t.*

kasraħ: as *i* in *bit*.
ḍammaħ: as *u* as in *put*.

The three long vowels of Arabic are:
ا following a letter carrying a *fatḥaħ*: *ā* as *a* in *father*.
ي following a letter carrying a *kasraħ*: *ī* as *i* in *machine*.
و following a letter carrying a *ḍammaħ*: *ū* as *u* in *rule*.

(c) The Diphthongs
The two diphthongs of Arabic are:
وْ following a letter carrying a *fatḥaħ*: *aw* as *ow* in *town*, not as *aw* in *claw*.
يْ following a letter carrying a *fatḥaħ*: *ay* as *i* in *bite*, not as *ay* in *bay*.

*****

NOTES ON THE NON-ENGLISH LETTERS OCCURRING IN THE BOOK

ă (Rumanian): the neutral vowel as *a* in *above*.
ã (Portuguese): a nasalized *a*.
å (Swedish and Danish): as *o* in *hot*.
ä (German and Swedish): *e* as in *bed*, but longer.

ë (Albanian): the neutral vowel as *a* in *above*.

ı (Turkish): *u* pronounced without rounding of the lips.

ø (Danish): *e* pronounced with rounded lips as *ö* in the German *Löwe*.

ü (German and Turkish): *i* pronounced with rounded lips.

ç (French and Portuguese): *s*. This letter is used instead of *c* when it is followed by *a, o or u*.

ć (Serbo-Croatian): as *ch* in the German *ich*, but preceded by a *t*.

ş (Turkish and Rumanian): as *sh* in *she*.

ś (Polish): as *ch* in the German *ich*.

š (Serbo-Croatian): as *sh* in *she*.

ž (Serbo-Croatian): as *s* in *measure*. I have used this symbol in the transliteration of some Persian and Russian words also.

ł (Polish): as *w* in *we*.

n̲ (Sanskrit): a retroflex *n*.

l' (Russian): a palatalized *l*.

t' (Russian): a palatalized *t*.

χ phonetic symbol representing *ch* as in the Scotch *loch* or the German *Buch*.

* An asterisk placed before a word signifies a hypothetical form.

* * * * *

NOTES ON WRITING ARABIC & OTHER FOREIGN WORDS

The immediate Arabic source of a word is written in bold roman type followed by the same word written in Arabic letters. Arabic words in other contexts are written in italics, e.g. *Syrup* is from the Arabic **šarāb** (شَرَاب), a drink, which is derived from *šariba*, to drink.

Words from languages using non-Latin letters are first written in italic Latin letters followed by the same words written in their own letters, e.g. Greek *bakales* (μπακαλης), Russian *bakal* (бакал).

* * * * *

ACKNOWLEDGEMENTS

I wish to point out that I have taken most of the quotations from the *OED* online version, and some from the compact edition of 1980. Readers desirous of more information about the authors and their titles are advised to refer to *OED*.

In conclusion, I desire to express my sincere

thanks to Br Khalid Raheem of Toronto, who not
only meticulously edited and proofread the
manuscript, but also made valuable suggestions
for improving various aspects of the book. My
thanks are also due to Br Ṣāliḥ al-Nawwār of
Madinah who did most of the typesetting, and to
Br Abubakar Muhammad Sani of Nigeria who
did the indexing. *Jazāhumu-llāhu khayrā.*[1]

---

1 Arabic for 'May Allah reward them!'

CHAPTER 1
HISTORY

Eric: You speak Arabic, Ahmad. Don't you?

Ahmad: Yes, I do. And so does every Englishman. In fact all Europeans speak Arabic.

Eric: What do you mean by this strange statement?

Ahmad: I mean that English and other European languages have so many important Arabic words in them, that one can almost say that Europeans speak Arabic.

Eric: Please tell me what important Arabic words we use in English. I do not want you to mention words like *fatwa, intifada, jihad, sunnah, shia, sharia, fedayeen*, etc. These are foreign elements, and in no way constitute a part of our language. I want you to mention words which look English, smell English, taste English, and are steeped in English history and culture, or represent scientific facts. I am sure you will not be able to do that.

Ahmad: Here is a word that seems to have been created specially to meet all your requirements:

it looks English, smells English and tastes English, and is steeped in British history, and comes right from the heart of London.

Eric: What is it?

Ahmad: *Trafalgar!*

Eric: You mean to say *Trafalgar* is Arabic. Are you kidding?

Ahmad: No, I am not.

Eric: I will not accept any of your pronouncements unless you prove them beyond a shadow of a doubt, and corroborate your claims with linguistic evidence.

Ahmad: That is exactly what I propose to do. So are you ready to listen?

Eric: Yes. Go ahead, please.

Ahmad: Now, this word has a bit of both history and geography. *Trafalgar Square* houses the monument of Lord Nelson, the hero of the Battle of Trafalgar which was fought west of Cape Trafalgar in Spain. Like many Spanish place-names, *Trafalgar* is also Arabic. It is the Europeanized form of the Arabic **al-ṭaraf al-agharr** (الطرف الأغرّ) literally meaning 'the Shining End'.

Eric: If that is the history of this word, it may be Arabic.

Ahmad: And it is. This word has also other

meanings. A type of stage-coach is called Trafalgar. William Thackeray says, 'Whither ... is the light four-inside Trafalgar coach carrying us?'[1]

Likewise, a type size is called Trafalgar. This is one size larger than the two-line double pica, and one size smaller than canon.

Eric: Anything more about *Trafalgar*?

Ahmad: Well, I am thinking of the hero of the Battle of Trafalgar, Admiral Horatio Nelson.

Eric: You seem to be suggesting that *admiral* is Arabic.

Ahmad: Exactly.

Eric: I should be cautious with you now. I am afraid you can turn any English word into Arabic.

Ahmad: I don't have a magic wand to turn any English word into Arabic, nor do I have the gift of the gab. I only have hard facts: linguistic facts that speak for themselves.

Eric: O.K. Let me hear what you have to say about *admiral*.

Ahmad: *Admiral* was formerly without the *d*, i.e. *amiral*. In a 1460 passage we read, 'The Erl of Arundel, Richard, was mad amyrel of the se.'[2] The French form of the word is also without the

---

1 *Vanity Fair*, vii.
2 John Capgrave, *The Chronicle of England*, 250.

d (*amiral*). So also is the case in Swedish and Rumanian. Italian has *ammiraglio*.

Now, this word *amiral* is from the Arabic **amīr al-baḥr** (أمير البحر), the commander of the sea, or **amīr al-mā'** (أميرُ الماء), the commander of the waters. In such expressions, the Arabic definite article **al-** prefixed to the second word was wrongly thought to be part of the first word, and so was suffixed to it creating a new word, *amiral*.

Eric: Where did the *d* come from in the English *admiral*?

Ahmad: That is a very good question. A foreign word has no etymology in the language it has been borrowed into. And people want to connect the foreign word to words already known to them. The result is what is known as folk etymology. In the case of *amiral*, people related it to the Latin *admirabilis* meaning wonderful, and changed *amiral* to *admiral*.

This distorted English form of the word has entered other European languages as well: it is *Admiral* in German, *admiraal* in Dutch, *admirał* in Polish, and *admiral* (адмирал) in Russian.

Eric: That is really interesting.

CHAPTER 2
MATHEMATICS

Ahmad: You also wanted to have examples of Arabic words denoting scientific facts. Could there have been any scientific progress without the concept of zero?

Eric: No, of course not. Do you want to say that *zero* is also Arabic?

Ahmad: Yes. The Arabic system of enumeration which Europe adopted in the 9th century had a magical element called the *cipher*. This represents the Arabic şifr (صِفر) literally meaning empty.[1] When the Italians took this word into their language, they made two changes in the word. First, they replaced the initial *s* with a *z*, probably because their *z*, which is pronounced *ts*[2], is closer to the Arabic letter ṣād (ص) than the simple *s*. Secondly, they added an *o* at the end of the word to give it an Italian look as all their

---

1 From the verb ṣafira yaṣfaru (i-a group), to be empty. *OED* has ṣafara which is wrong.

2 Remember the ubiquitous Italian *pizza* which is pronounced *peetsa*?

masculine nouns and adjectives have this termination, e.g. *bravo, generalissimo!* After these two cosmetic operations, the Italianized Arabic word became *zifero.* But the word did not survive this twin operation, and soon disintegrated. Two of its six letters fell off. What remained is *zero.* This shortened form of the word waxed so strong that it travelled to every nook and cranny of the world, and you will hardly find one who does not know or use it.

Eric: That means that *zero* and *cipher* are one and the same word!

Ahmad: Exactly. Initially the Arabic system of enumeration was used only by the scientists. Hence the word *cipher* acquired the meaning of a secret language, or a code. To *decipher* originally meant to decode, but later came to mean to read or interpret secret, unknown, or difficult writing.

As we are discussing a mathematical term, let me give you another very important word pertaining to this field. It is *algebra.* The mathematician Abū Jaᶜfar Muḥammad ibn Mūsā al-Khwārizmi, who originated this branch of mathematics, called it in Arabic *al-jabr wa l-muqābalaħ,* the science of redintegration and equation. The first word **al-jabr**[1] (الجَبْر), which literally means resetting of broken or dislocated bones, metaphorically means redintegration. In the early 13th century, this word was taken into Italian as *algebra* (in Spanish and Portuguese, *álgebra*) whence it came to English. The French form has dropped the final *a* (*algèbre*). Most European languages have the Italian form with the final *a*. In Russian, it is *algebra* (алгебра). Even modern Greek uses this same word *algebra* (αλγεβρα). Albanian has the French form (*algjebër*), and does not end in *a*.

The second part of its Arabic name **al-muqābalah** (الْمُقَابَلَة) was also used in English to denote this science in the form of *almachabel*. A 1570 text reads, 'The Science of workyng Algiebar and Almachabel, that is, the Science of findyng an vnknowen number, by Addyng of a Number, and Diuision and æquation'[2], but this word is now obsolete.

It is to be noted that the word *algebra* is also used in English in its original sense of bonesetting. A 1541 text says, 'The helpes of Algebra

---

[1] *OED* writes the word with an *e* (*al-jebr*). The correct spelling is *al-jabr*.

[2] John Dee, *Math. Præf.*, 6.

& of dislocations'.[1] Another text from 1565
states, 'This Araby worde Algebra sygnifyeth as
well fractures of bones, etc. as sometyme the
restauration of the same.'[2] Though this meaning
is obsolete in English, it is still in vogue in
Spanish.

Eric: What is the Spanish word?

Ahmad: It is the same word *álgebra* which means
both algebra and the art of setting joints. And
algebrista means algebraist as well as bone-setter.

Eric: That is very interesting.

Ahmad: The name of al-Khwārizmi has left its
trace in *algorism* meaning the Arabic, or decimal
system of numeration. A 1549 text says, 'Other
men stande for no more than Ciphres in
Algorisme'.[3]

In an attempt to derive it from the Greek
arithmos (αριθμος) meaning number, it is also
spelt *algorithm*. In French, it has only this spelling (*algorithme*). The Spanish and Portuguese
spelling *algoritmo* betrays the same pseudo-
etymology.

It should be noted here that the Spanish
guarismo meaning figure, digit, cipher is the

---

1 Robert Copland, *Guydon's Formulary.*
2 John Halle, *Hist. Expost.*, 19.
3 Sir Thomas Chaloner, *Erasmi Moriae Encomium.*

same as *algorism*, but without the Arabic definite article **al-**.

The present-day computer language ALGOL is an acronym for ***algorithmic language***.

Eric: That was a very long but interesting exposition. What is your next word?

Ahmad: As we are discussing mathematical terms, I would like to mention here a term which is not Arabic, but is the translation of an Arabic term. It is *sine* which is one of the three trigonometrical functions. The Arabic word is **jayb** (جَيْب) which literally means the bosom of a shirt. This was translated by the Latin word *sinus* meaning, *inter alia*, the fold of the toga about the breast. This Arabic word in the trigonometrical sense is in fact an adaptation of the Sanskrit word *jīvā* (जीवा) which means the chord of an arc.

CHAPTER 3
ASTRONOMY

Eric: What next?

Ahmad: We spoke a short while ago about ALG-OL. That reminds me of the astronomical *Algol.*

Eric: I suppose that is the name of a star.

Ahmad: Exactly.

Eric: But is that an Arabic word?

Ahmad: Yes, it is. I will tell the whole story. Algol is the second brightest star in the constellation Perseus which is supposed to represent Perseus holding the Gorgon Medusa's head after killing her. Algol represents Medusa's head which in Arabic is called **ra's al-ghūl** (رَأْسُ الغُول) meaning the demon's head. European languages left out the first part of the name, and changed the second part **al-ghūl** to *Algol.*

Eric: Is this word related to *ghoul?*

Ahmad: Yes, it is the same word without the article **al-**. It is thought to be a demon that preys on human corpses. James Lowell says, 'It sucks with the vampire, gorges with the ghoule.'[1] We also speak of *ghoulish.* Mary Braddon says, 'They had done nothing but talk about the murder all the morning with a ghoulish gusto.'[2]

Eric: Do we have other star names of Arabic origin in English?

Ahmad: Quite a lot. Paul Kunitzsch lists 210 star names of Arabic origin in his *Arabische Sternnamen In Europa*[3] (Arabic Star Names in Europe). One could say that the skies are full of Arabic writing.

Eric: Could you give me a couple of examples?

Ahmad: Yes, of course. *Vega* is the brightest star in the constellation Lyra (α Lyrae). This word is a corruption of its Arabic name (*al-nasr al-*) wāqi‘ (النَّسْرُ الواقِعُ), literally meaning the swooping eagle which in Arabic astronomy is the name of an asterism comprising α, ε and ζ Lyrae.

Vega is one of the oldest Arabic star names applied in the West, from the end of the 10th century CE.[4]

Another important star name is *Aldebran* which is a first-magnitude red star in the constel-

---

1 *Among My Books*, Ser. i (1873) 84.
2 *Strange World*, I. ix. 150.
3 Published by Otto Harrassowitz, Wiesbaden, 1959.
4 Paul Kunitzsch, *Short Guide To Modern Star Names And Their Derivations*, p. 44.

lation Taurus (α Tauri). William Roscoe Thayer says,

> ... I saw on a minaret's tip
> Aldebran like a ruby aflame, then leisurely slip
> In the black horizon's bowl.[1]

It is from the Arabic name **al-dabarān** (الدَّبَران) which literally means the follower, i.e. of the Pleiades. It is also one of the oldest Arabic star names applied in the West, from the end of the 10th century CE.[2]

The third star name I propose to mention is *Betelgeuse*, or *Betelgeuze*, a reddish first-magnitude star in Orion's shoulder (α Orionis). It is from **yad al-jawzā'** (يَدُ الْجَوزاء), i.e. the hand of Orion. In the medieval Latin transliteration, it became *bedalgeuze* with a *b* instead of the original *y* as these two letters have identical forms in Arabic and differ only in the number of dots (ب *b* with one dot and ي *y* with two). Later it was thought to be from the Arabic **ibṭ al-jawzā'** (إبْطُ الْجَوْزاء), i.e. the armpit of Orion, and so the *d* was changed to *t* giving rise to the present day *betelgeuze*.[3]

---

1 Richard Hinckley Allen, *Star Names, Their Lore And Meaning*, p. 385.
2 *Short Guide To Modern Star Names*, pp. 45-46.
3 *CTCD* says it is from the Arabic *bayt-al-jawzā'*, which is not correct.

Eric: That was concentrated erudition. I hope your next words will be fit for ordinary mortals.

Ahmad: I was thinking of dealing with some more star names like *Achernar, Alpheratz, Azelfafage, Benetnasch, Denebola, Dschubba, Fomalhaut, Menkalinan, Rasalgethi, Sadalmelik, Toliman, Unukalhai, Wezen, Zubenelgenubi, Zubeneschamali,* etc., but as you want words fit for ordinary mortals, I propose to give you some astronomical terms of Arabic origin which lay-men also use.

Eric: I hope they are not jaw-breakers and tongue-twisters like the ones you have just mentioned.

Ahmad: No. The word I am going to tell you about is a sleek and beautiful word. It is *zenith.* In astronomy, it means the point in the sky directly above an observer, and metaphorically is applied to the highest point of achievement. It is an abbreviation of the Arabic expression **samt al-ra's**[1] (سَمْتُ الرّأس), i.e. the direction of the head. The word **samt** became *cenit(h)* in old French. In modern French, it is *zénith* whence comes the English *zenith.* In Spanish, it is *cenit,* in Italian

---

1 *OED* (under *zenith*) writes it *samt ar-rās* with a long *a* and without the sign of the *hamzah,* which is permissible. But under *azimuth,* it writes *samt ar-rāʾs* with the long *a* and the *hamzah,* which is not correct.

zinit, and in Portuguese zênite. In German, Dutch, and Swedish, it is zenit. The Russian zenit (зенит) is obviously from German and the modern Greek zenith (ζενιθ) is from English. Etymologically related to this word is azimuth which is also an astronomical term meaning an angle corresponding to a distance around the earth's horizon, and it is from the Arabic al-sumūt (السُّمُوت) meaning directions. It is the plural of samt which we have just met in zenith.

Now, the opposite of zenith is nadir which means the part of the sky directly below an observer, and metaphorically means the lowest point. Henry Hallam says, 'The seventh century is the nadir of the human mind in Europe.'[1] Thomas Hardy says, 'Its transcendental aspirations ... based on the geocentric view of things, a zenithal paradise, a nadiral hell.'[2] The word nadir is from the Arabic naẓīr (نظير) meaning matching, corresponding, opposite.

Even the name of the great astronomical treatise of Ptolemy in Greek appears in English in its Arabic form donning the Arabic definite article al-, Almagest. Chaucer says,

---

1 *Introduction to the Literature of Europe in the 15th, 16th and 17th Centuries,* I. i. 5.
2 *Tess,* II. xxv. 56.

His almageste and bokes gret and smale,
His astrelabre longing for his art.[1]

The word comes from its Arabic name **al-majasṭī**[2] (المَجَسْطِي) which is the Greek *megiste* (μεγιστη) with the Arabic definite article **al-**. The Greek word means the greatest, and was applied to the great treatise of Ptolemy Μαθηματικη συνταξις in contradistinction to the elementary works studied before it.

Eric: We have been soaring high into the heavens for quite some time. Shall we come down to earth now and speak about more mundane matters?

Ahmad: Very well, but please let me first speak about three more words pertaining to astronomy.

Eric: Please go ahead.

Ahmad: The first is *alidad* or *alidade* which is a revolving index for reading the graduations of an astrolabe, quadrant, or similar instrument. It is from the Arabic **al-ʿiḍādah** (العِضَادة) meaning the same. The Spanish and Portuguese *alidada* is very close to the Arabic original. French as usual

---

1 Miller's *Tale*, 22.
2 This word is written with a ط, and the ج has a *fatḥah* as in *Tāj al-ʿArūs*, but *OED* writes it with a ت, and vocalizes the ج with a *kasrah*.

dropped the final syllable, thus reducing the word to *alidade* which is the source of the English form. Here I must correct a mistake occurring in *Le Petit Robert* which gives the Arabic original as *al-idhāla* with an *l* which is wrong.

Eric: The second?

Ahmad: My second word is *almacantar*, which has many alternate spellings. It is used in the plural and means small circles of sphere parallel to the horizon, cutting the meridian at equal distances. Chaucer says, 'The almykanteras in thin astrelabie ben compownet by two & two, where-as some Almykanteras in sondri Astrelabies ben compownet by on and no.'[1]
It is from the Arabic **al-muqanṭar** (المُقَنْطَر) meaning a sundial.

Eric: But the word seems to be obsolete.

Ahmad: Yes, indeed it is. But some want to revive it. Listen to what S. Chandler has to say. He says, 'I propose to call the instrument [for the determination of time and altitude] the 'Almacantar', from an Arabic astronomical term, now obsolete in its general use.'[2]

Eric: I hope it has been revived, and I will have

1 *A Treatise on the Astrolabe*, II.§ 5.
2 *Scientific Observer*, III. No5. 36.

occasion to use it some day. And now your third and last word.

Ahmad: My third word is *almury*, which has also to do with the astrolabe. It is the 'denticle' or tooth-like pointer situated on the rete of the astrolabe near the 'head' of Capricorn. Chaucer says, 'Thin almury is cleped the denticle of capricorne or else the kalkuler.[1]

Eric: You said 'on the rete of the astrolabe.' What does rete mean?

Ahmad: It is a metal plate affixed to an astrolabe that indicates the positions of the principal fixed stars.

Now for the etymology of *almury*. It is from the Arabic **al-murī** (المُري) literally meaning the indicator. It is the active participle of the Arabic verb *arā*, to show.[2]

Eric: Your third word sounds as dead as the dodo.

Ahmad: Yes, it is now dead, but there was a time when it was a living word, and it played an important role in the development of astronomy.

---

1 *A Treatise on the Astrolabe*, I. xxiii.
2 *OED* writes the Arabic word as *al-mur'ī* with a *hamzah*, which is wrong. In the fourth conjugation of *ra'ā*, the second radical, which is *hamzah*, is lost resulting in *arā* for the original *ar'ā*, and the active participle is *muri(n)*, *al-murī*.

Eric: I suppose you are right. Shall we now move on to another domain?

CHAPTER 4
AMENITIES

Ahmad: Our next domain is amenities. You said you wanted to move on to more mundane matters, didn't you?

Eric: Yes, I did.

Ahmad: Let's begin with *mattress.*

Eric: Is *mattress* Arabic? What did we sleep on before we got it from the Arabs?

Ahmad: I do not know. What I know for sure is that *mattress* comes from the Arabic **miṭraḥ** (مطرَح) meaning a quilted cushion. The English form comes from the old French *materas* (which has now become *matelas* in modern French). Italian has *materasso.*

Another form with the Arabic definite article **al-** is found in some other languages. The closest to the Arabic form is *almatrac* in Provençal. The Spanish *almadraque* is now obsolete.

German *Matraze*, Dutch *matras*, Danish *madras* and Swedish *madrass* are all from the French form. The Russian form *matrats* (матрац) is obviously from German. So also is the Polish *materac* (pronounced *materats*).

Now, let us get up from the quilted cushion, and recline on a sofa.

Eric: Do you want to say that *sofa* too is Arabic?

Ahmad: That is what the linguistic evidence says. *Sofa* is from the Arabic ṣuffah (صُفّة) which in late Arabic means a narrow masonry bench. In classical Arabic, however, it meant a spacious parlour in the house. Such a parlour existed in the Prophet's Mosque in Madīnah where some poor companions of the Prophet Muḥammad lived. It had masonry platforms for sitting. The modern meaning of the word has been coloured by this historical fact. This parlour was called *al-Ṣuffah*, and those who lived therein were known as *Ahl al-Ṣuffah*.

The word is used in many of the European languages. It is spelt just as it is in English[1] except in Swedish where it is *soffa*. In Russian and Mecedonian, it is *sofa* (софа).

I think it is time for a hot cup of coffee.

Eric: You seem to be suggesting that *coffee* is Arabic. Am I correct?

Ahmad: Yes, you are correct. The word *coffee* ultimately comes from the Arabic qahwah (قَهْوَة).

---

1 In Italian, it is spelt *sofà* and in Spanish and Portuguese, *sofá*.

Originally meaning loss of appetite, it was applied to wine in classical Arabic, and to coffee in later times. The Turkish form of the word *kahve* became *caffè* in Italian, *café* in French, Spanish and Portuguese, *Kaffee* in German, *kaffe* in Swedish and Danish, *cafea* in Rumanian and *kafes* (καφες) in modern Greek. All these forms have *a* after the first letter as in the original Arabic. But the Dutch *kofie*, English *coffee* and Russian *kofe* (кофе) have *o* representing an earlier *au* which developed from the combination *ahv* of the Turkish form.

   Cafeteria meaning a self-service restaurant in a factory or a college is an American Spanish word for a coffee shop, and is derived from the Spanish *cafetero* meaning café owner.

Eric: What about *mocha*? Is it also Arabic?

Ahmad: Yes, it is. It was originally produced in Yemen, and was named after the Yemeni port of Mocha (المُخَا) on the Red Sea whence it was exported. In *Divry's Modern English-Greek and Greek-English Dictionary* (New York, 1971), *mocha* is explained as καφες της Μεκκας (coffee from Mecca) which is, of course, wrong.

   Arabic not only gave Europe coffee, but also the coffee pot. Though English has not availed itself of this offer, some European languages

have. Italian has *bricco* meaning a coffee pot,
teapot, kettle, and modern Greek has *briki*
(μπρικι) meaning a small coffee pot. Polish has
transferred it to tea, for *imbryk* in Polish is a
teapot or a teakettle. The Rumanian *ibric*
meaning a teakettle or coffee pot has preserved
the Arabic form of the word which is **ibrīq** (اِبْرِيق)
meaning a flask or a flagon, and in its plural
form *abārīq*, it is used in the Qur᾽ān (56:18) in
the context of the pleasures of paradise.

From the way you are holding your head, you
seem to be suffering from a headache.

Eric: Yes, I am, but don't tell me that *headache* is
also Arabic.

Ahmad: No, *headache* is not Arabic, but the cure
for headache is Arabic.

Eric: What do you mean by that?

Ahmad: The Arabic word for headache is **ṣudāʿ**
(صُدَاع) which passed into medieval Latin in the
form of *sodanum*, and was applied to glasswort
which, because of its soda content, was used as a
remedy for headache. Later it came to mean
sodium carbonate as it is contained in glasswort.
Soda water is a good drink, and is among the
amenities we are talking about.

Eric: So our *soda* is from the Arabic *ṣudāʿ*
meaning headache?

Ahmad: Exactly.

Eric: And also the chemical term *sodium*?

Ahmad: Yes.

Eric: Languages play with words and their meanings.

Ahmad: And history is their playmate.

CHAPTER 5
ENTERTAINMENT AND AMUSEMENT

Eric: Has Arabic given us any words in the field of entertainment or amusement?

Ahmad: Yes, certainly. One such word is *lute*, a stringed musical instrument played like a guitar. Keats says,

> Thy lute-voiced brother will I sing ere long.[1]

It is from the Arabic **al-ʿūd** (العُود) meaning the same. The immediate source of the English word is the old French *lut*, which in modern French has become *luth*. The Spanish form is *laúd*. In Italian, it is *liuto*, and *liutio* is the maker of the lute and other stringed instruments. The Portuguese form *alaúd* has preserved the Arabic definite article intact. German has *Laute*, Dutch *luit*, Swedish *luta* and Danish *lut*. Even modern Greek has it in the form of *lavuton* (λαβουτον).

Macedonian has *lauta* (лаута), and Serbo-Croatian *leut*. Some Slovak forms have *nya* at the end of the word as the Russian *lyutnya* (лютня),

---

1 *Endymion*, iv. 774.

and the Polish *lutnia*.

Eric: I am pretty sure Arabic could not have given us many words in this field, i.e. the field of entertainment and amusement.

Ahmad: You are not quite right in your assumption, Eric. I am going to give you now a very important word which, though belonging to the field of amusement, has generated quite a few words belonging to other fields as well. It is such an important European word that I am afraid you might refuse to accept its Arabic origin.

Eric: Let me first of all know what it is.

Ahmad: It is the word *chess*.

Eric: How can *chess* be Arabic, Ahmad? It doesn't have **al-**, and is *ch* an Arabic sound?

Ahmad: Not all Arabic words don **al-**. And speech sounds undergo numerous changes during their long voyages from one language to another.

Now let me tell you the 'chequered' history of *chess*. Chess is an Indian game, and its Sanskrit name is *chaturanga* (चतुरंग) which literally means four-membered, and is applied to a complete army consisting of infantry, cavalry, chariots and elephants. This Sanskrit word became *šatrang* (شترنگ) in Persian. Arabic took it from Persian, and to fit it into its phonetic system, changed it to **šaṭranj** (شَطْرَنْج) meaning chess.

This Arabic word is found only in three European languages: in Portuguese, Spanish and modern Greek. In the first, it is *xadrez*. It is to be remembered that in Portuguese and earlier Spanish, *x* is pronounced *sh*. In *xadrez* the *n* has been dropped, and the *j* has become *z*. The initial *a* in the earlier Spanish form *axedrez* points to the Arabic definite article **al-** which you were looking for. In present-day Spanish, the word is spelt with a *j* (*ajedrez*). In modern Spanish, *j* is a voiceless velar fricative like the *ch* in the German *Buch*, or the Scottish *loch*.

From the Portuguese *xadrez* is derived *xadrezar* meaning to chequer, and *xadrezado* meaning chequered. And from the Spanish *ajedrez* come *ajedrezar*, to chequer, *ajedrezado*, chequered, and *ajedrezamiento*, chequer-work.

The third European language which has this word is modern Greek where it is *zatrikion* (ζατρικιον). Here also, the *n* has been lost, for the original form should have been *zatrinkion*. As Greek has no *sh*, it has changed it to *z*.

The chess king is **al-šāh** (الشَّاه) in Arabic.[1] It is one of the chess terms Arabic borrowed from

---

1 Remember the Shah of Iran?

Persian. And this is the word that gave many European languages their name for the game of chess.

The Arabic *al-šāh* became **eschac* in old French, which later was modified to *eschès* and *eschèc*. By dropping the initial *e* from the first form, English got its *chess*.

The word *šāh* was also used by chess players to warn their opponents that their king is under threat. In this sense, English took the second French form after dropping the initial *e*, so it became *check*.

Eric: That means that *chess* and *check* are twins.

Ahmad: Exactly. We may call them 'Arabic twins' in line with 'Siamese twins'. Now let's see the semantic development of the word *check*. In chess, as *check* involved slowing or stopping the movement of the king, it acquired meanings like slowing, stopping, controlling, verification. In the last sense, it was also applied to the counterfoil of a bank bill. Dr Johnson defines it as 'the correspondent cipher of a bank bill.'[1] Later it came to mean a document containing an account holder's order to the bank to pay a sum of money from his or her account to another person. When the check became such a powerful

---

1 *OED, cheque.*

instrument of monetary transaction, the British gave it a dignified look by changing its spelling to *cheque.* The Americans, who are practical in their approach, have let it retain its old spelling.

Eric: How interesting it is to note that *cheque* comes from *šāh*!

Ahmad: Let's now see how French dealt with these two words.

We have seen that old French had two forms of the same word, *eschès* and *eschèc.* English made use of both: the first for the game, and the second for the warning delivered to the king. Modern French uses only the second word which has now become *échec.*

Eric: How does it differentiate between the two meanings?

Ahmad: It uses the plural form (*les échecs*) for the game, and the singular form for *check.* Here is another very important observation. The English looked at the bright side of *check,* and ascribed to it meanings like examination and verification, which resulted in the birth of the millionaire word *cheque.* The French on the other hand looked at the dark side of *check,* and ascribed to it negative meanings like failure, defeat, loss.

Eric: This is really an interesting subject.

Ahmad: Yes, and you will soon come across more interesting revelations. If a king is in a position in which it can neither be protected nor moved out of check, the winning player says **al-šāh māt** (الشّاه مَاتَ), i.e. the king is dead. This Arabic expression became *checkmate* in English.

It is interesting to note that this Arabic word became *šakhmat*[1] (шахматы) in Russian, and means chess.[1] *Checkmate* in Russian is шах и мат, i.e. check and mate.

Mate alone is also used in the sense of *checkmate* as in 'The Church-men or Prelates checked them often, but could never give them the mate.'[2] As checkmate in chess involves total defeat, the word *mate* acquired the meaning of dull and lustreless. But in this sense, it is spelt *mat, matt,* or *matte* as in 'a gloss or a matt finish.'

Connected with this word is also the archaic *amate*[3] meaning to dismay, dishearten, cast down as in Keats' 'A half-blown flow'ret which cold blasts amate.'[4]

Eric: When are you moving me out of check?

---

1 The modern Hebrew *šakhmāṭ* (שַׁחְמָט) for chess comes from this Russian word.
2 Nathaniel Bacon, *Historical Discourse of the Uniformity of the Government of England,* I. xvi (1739) 32.
3 *CTCD.*
4 *Life, Letters and Literary Remains,* I. 12 (1848).

Ahmad: I am afraid it will take some time. *Check* has checked our progress.

One more word connected with chess is *exchequer*.

Eric: Is *exchequer* also Arabic? What have you left for the English language, then?

Ahmad: Don't worry. The richness of English lies in its diversity.

Now, let us go back to *exchequer*. In middle English, it was spelt *escheker*, and is from the old French *exschequier* meaning chessboard. Later it came to mean the Treasury, or the ministry of finance in Britain.

Eric: But what magic wand transformed the chessboard into the ministry of finance?

Ahmad: The magic wand was the semantic process combined with a bit of British history. The word *exchequer* originally referred to the table covered with a cloth divided into squares like the chessboard on which the accounts of the revenue were kept by means of counters. Later the word came to mean the Treasury itself.

Eric: What a turn of fortune for *exchequer*!

Ahmad: At the beginning of our talk, you insisted that I give you a word steeped in British history. Does this satisfy you?

Eric: It sure does. Here is an Arabic word soaked

in British history. Are we finished with *chess*?

Ahmad: No, not yet. With the omission of the initial *ex* from *exchequer*, we got *chequer*, or *checker* meaning chessboard, chessboard pattern, alternation of colours as on a chessboard, etc. But this word is better known to us as a verb meaning a) to mark in squares of varying colours as in 'a chequered blanket'[1], b) to variegate, alternate, etc. as in 'a chequered history, or career or past.' Shakespeare says,

> The gray ey'd morne ...
> Checkring the Easterne Clouds with
> streakes of light.[2]

Before I close the chequered history of *chess*, I would like to point to one more meaning of *chequer*. It also meant to deposit money in an exchequer, then metaphorically, it came to mean to treasure up. John Davies says, 'There ... Nature chequers up all gifts of grace.'[3]

Eric: Ahmad, you haven't told me the name of chess in other European languages.

Ahmad: I was so preoccupied with *check* and its semantic development, and how a chequered

---

1 *Check* is also used in this sense as in 'sweet kerchief check'd with heavenly blue.' (George Canning, *Anti-Jacobin, Rovers*).
2 *Romeo and Juliet*, II. iii. 2.
3 *Wittes Pilgrimage*, (1876) 32 (D).

piece of cloth created the British ministry of finance, that I forgot to tell you how chess is called in some other European languages.

The German word for chess is *Schach* which is very close to the original Arabic *šāh*. It is also called *Schachspiel*, i.e. the game of *šāh*. In Dutch, it is *schaak* or *schaakspel*. Serbo-Croatian, Rumanian and Albanian use the Arabic word *šāh* without any change, but its spelling differs from one language to another. Serbo-Croatian writes it *šāh*, Rumanian writes it *şah* and Albanian writes it *shah* in plain Latin letters.

Eric: Are we now bidding farewell to *chess* and *check*?

Ahmad: Yes, we are.

Eric: I hope your next word will have no chequered history. It will have a simpler meaning, and its exposition will not take as much time, though I fully enjoyed every word of the story of chess.

Ahmad: I have a word exactly answering to your specifications. But it will take us out of England to East Africa. It is *safari* which means a trip to see or hunt wild animals, especially in East Africa. One is said *to go on safari*, or *to be on safari*. It is the Arabic word **safar** (سَفَر) meaning journey, but has come to English through

Swahili.[1] The word is used in many European languages.

Eric: This word seems to have more geography than history.

Ahmad: You are right. My next word has a bit of history. It is *hazard*.

Eric: You seem to forget that we are now discussing words dealing with entertainment and amusement. How does *hazard* fit in here?

Ahmad: It fits in here perfectly. Its history will tell you how.

Hazard is originally a game at dice in which the chances are complicated by a number of arbitrary rules.[2] A 1778 text states, 'The Game of Hazard ... may be played by any Number of Persons.'[3] From this came the other meanings of chance, venture, risk, peril.

This word is from the Arabic **al-zahr** (الزَّهْر) meaning dice. It became *azar* in Spanish where it means unfortunate card or throw at dice, unforeseen disaster, accident, disappointment. Portuguese also has the same form, and it means misfortune, bad luck, mishap. *Jogo de azar*

---

1 *Le Petit Robert* says that it is from the Arabic *safora* meaning to journey. This is not right. To journey is *safara*, and more frequently *sāfara*.

2 *OED*.

3 Charles Jones, *Hoyle's Games Improved*, 209.

means game of chance. In Italian, it is *azzardo* and means risk; and *giuoco d'azzardo* means game of chance.

From Spanish, it passed into old French in the 17th century in the form of *hasart* whence came the English form *hazard*. In modern French, it is *hasard*.

In Germanic languages, the word means gambling or game of chance. It is *Hasardspiel* in German, *hazardspel* in Dutch, *hasardspel* in Swedish and *hasardspil* in Danish.

In Serbo-Croatian, *hazardan* means both risky and gambling. *Hazardne igre* means game of chance.

In Macedonian, *khazardna igra* (хазардна игра) means game of chance.

In Russian, *azartnay igra* (азартная игра) means game of chance. But *azart* (азарт) means ardour, excitement, passion, etc. as a game of chance is played to the accompaniment of these.

Eric: Let's leave this hazardous path, and walk to safety. Give me a word dealing with modern life. Don't you have a word pertaining to sports?

Ahmad: Do you play tennis?

Eric: Yes, I do.

Ahmad: So you should know the origin of *racket*. It is originally from the Arabic **rāḥah** (رَاحة)

meaning the palm of the hand. In English, *racket* comes from the French *raquette*. In 14th century French, it was written *rachete*, and meant palm of the hand.[1] In modern French, it means a racket and also snowshoe, as it does in English also. The French form is from the Italian *racchetta*. In Spanish, it is *raqueta*, in Portuguese *raquete*, in German *Rakett*, in Dutch *raket*, in Swedish *racket*, in Russian *raketka* (ракетка), in Serbo-Croatian *reket*.

As a boy you must have put on masks.

Eric: Yes, I did. Why? Is *mask* Arabic?

Ahmad: Yes, it is. It is from **maskharah** (مَسْخَرة), i.e. a laughingstock, a buffoon, and it is derived from the verb *sakhira* (سَخِرَ), to mock. It acquired the meaning of mask as buffoons cover their faces with masks. The word passed into Romance languages with a form very close to that of Arabic. In Spanish, *máscara* means masker, masquerader, a person in a mask. It also means mask, disguise, fancy-dress masquerade; pretence. From the idea of face cover, it has also come to mean a bandage.

In Italian, it is *maschera*, and means mask, masked man; disguise; face-guard (in fencing).

---

1 *Le Petit Robert.*

Mascheramento means concealment, camouflage, and *mascherata* means masquerade. The Portuguese, *mascara* also means a mask as well as a masker.

In French, the last two syllables -*ara* were lost, and the word became *masque* whence comes the English *masque* which means a masked person, a company of people wearing masks, a masked ball. *Mask* is a variant of *masque*, and originally meant a masked person as in the following text from Fielding's Tom Jones, 'This Mask was one of those ladies, who go to a masquerade only to vent ill-nature.'[1]

Masquerade, meaning an assembly of masked persons, generally at a ball, is from the Spanish *mascarada*.

In Swedish, it is *mask*, in German and Danish *maske*, and in Dutch *masker*.

In East European languages, it appears as *maska*: *maska* (маска) in Russian and Bulgarian, *maska* in Serbo-Croatian and Polish, *mască* in Rumanian.

In modern Greek, *maska* (μασκα), a mask, and *maskarata* (μασκαρατα), masquerade, are from the European source, but *mascaras* (μασκαρας), a buffoon, a trickster is from the

---

1 XIII, vii.

Turkish *maskara*, a buffoon, which is from the same Arabic word. The Greek *maskaraliki* (μασκαραλικι), mean trick, buffoonery, is from the Turkish *maskaralık*.

Eric: *Masquerade* now means to pretend as in 'A bitter enemy at heart, he masqueraded as a bosom friend and sympathizer.' Please tell me, is *mascara* of the eyelashes connected to this word?

Ahmad: Yes, of course. It is the same word, and the semantic connection between them is that *mascara* of the eyelashes is a sort of disguise just as putting on the mask is.

Here are two more words connected with *mask*. One of them is the architectural term *mascaron* meaning a grotesque face on a keystone, door-knocker, etc. The other is *mascot* meaning a person, an animal or a thing thought to bring good luck, and now every sports meet adopts a mascot. It is from the French *mascotte* which is from the Provençal *mascot*. This is a diminutive of *masco* which literally means a mask, but has now acquired the meaning of a sorcerer.[1]

Eric: Shall we unmask now?

Ahmad: Yes, but before we do that, we shall discuss a word which is closely related in meaning

---

1 *WNUUD.*

to *masquerade*, but is now obsolete. It is *matachin* which was a kind of sword-dancer in a fantastic costume, and also meant such a dance. Sir Philip Sidney says, 'Who euer sawe a matachin daunce to imitate fighting, this was a fight that did imitate the matachin: for they being but three that fought euerie one had (two) aduersaries.'[1]

It is believed to be from the Arabic **mutawajjihīn** (مُتَوجِّهِين), which is the accusative plural of *mutawajjih*, active participle of *tawajjaha*, to assume a mask, from *wajh*, face.[2]

The word became *matachín* in Spanish, and now means a laughingstock, buffoon; grotesque dance. It is *mattaccino* in Italian, and means a jester, mimic, strolling player.

Another word for a jester in Spanish is *moharrache*, *moharracho* from the Arabic **muharrij** (مُهَرِّج) meaning the same.

Eric: O.K. I think we have had enough amusement and entertainment. Can we now turn our attention to more serious business?

---

1 *Arcadia* (1590) I. xvii.
2 Reinhart Dozy, *Glossaire des mots espagnols et portuguais dérivés de l'arabe*, p. 309.

CHAPTER 6
TRADE

Ahmad: How about GATT?

Eric: Is there Arabic in GATT?

Ahmad: Yes, there is. The second T in GATT stands for *tariff* which is Arabic. Its Arabic original is **taʿrīf** (تَعْرِيف), and means notification. It is the infinitive of the second conjugation **ʿarrafa** (عَرَّف), to notify, make something known.[1]

It is *tarifa* in Spanish and Portuguese, *tariffa* in Italian, and *tarif* in French.

The word is found in most European languages. It is *Tarif* in German and Danish, *tarief* in Dutch, *tariff* in Swedish, *taryfa* in Polish, and *tarif* (тариф) in Russian.

Eric: Have you got any other word concerning trade?

Ahmad: My next word has to do with gold. It is the unit for measuring the purity of gold.

---

1 In *WNUUD* 'from *ʿarafa*, to inform'. This is wrong. *ʿarafa* means to know, and the second conjugation *ʿarrafa* means to inform. In *OED* 'عرف *ʿarafa* in 1ˢᵗ conj. to notify, make known'. This is also wrong.

Eric: Do you mean *carat*?

Ahmad: Exactly. It is from the Arabic qīrāṭ (قِيرَاط) with an *i* after the first letter, and means the same. The Spanish and Portuguese form have *i*. It is now *quilate* for the earlier *quirate*. In Spanish, the verb *quilatar* means to assay gold or silver. *Quilatera* means a pearl sieve.

Portuguese also has the verb *quilatar* with the same meaning. It also has the verbal noun *quilataçāo* meaning assaying, determination of weight. It also has *quilateira* which is an instrument for grading gems by size.

When the word arrived in Italy, its *i* changed to *a*, and the word became *carato*. The verb *caratare* not only means to weigh in carats, but also to examine minutely.

French as usual chopped off the final *-o* turning the word into *carat* and this is the source of the English word. All other languages have this English form.

It should be mentioned here that the Arabic word itself is a loan word from the Greek *keration* (κερατιον).

Eric: Before we finish with this golden word, I have a question for you. We have just seen that the Arabic *qīrāṭ* became *quilate* in Spanish and Portuguese, i.e. the Arabic *r* changed to *l*. Is there any other example of this kind of change?

Ahmad: Let me see... Please wait...Yes, there is. It is *quintal* meaning a hundredweight.

Eric: Is *quintal* Arabic?

Ahmad: Yes. It is from the Arabic qinṭār (قِنْطار) meaning the same and occurs in the Qurʾān twice, and once more in its plural form *qanāṭīr*. It became *quintale* (with an *l* in the place of *r*) in medieval Latin whence comes *quintal* in French, Spanish and Portuguese. It is *quintale* in Italian.

The word is found in its English form in Dutch where it is spelt *kwintaal*, and in Albanian which has *kuintal*.

Eric: After this digression let's go back to our subject, i.e. words dealing with trade.

Ahmad: O.K. My next word is *average*.

Eric: *Average?* What does it have to do with trade?

Ahmad: It may not have much to do with trade now, but it had its origin in maritime trade. The Arabic word ʿawār (عَوَار) means defect, and a defective commodity is called *silʿah dhāt ʿawār* (سِلْعَة ذاتُ عَوار). And ʿawāriyyah (عَوَارِيَّة) is a shipping term meaning goods damaged by sea water. This last word became *averia* in Spanish[1] and means damage sustained by merchandise during

---

[1] Hoad, *op. cit.,* Dozy, *op. cit.,* p. 217 where Dozy says, 'Il est très-certainement d'origine arabe.'

transport. In Italian, it is *avaria* and means damage at sea. In Portuguese also, it is *avaria* and means damage. As French does not favour the -*a* termination in nouns, it changed this word to *avarie*. Formerly, it meant damage to merchandise during sea transport, but now includes land and air transport as well.

In some European languages, the word has come to mean shipwreck, damage, breakdown, etc. In German, it is *Havarie*, in Danish *havari*, in Serbo-Croatian *havarija*, in Rumanian *avaria*, in Albanian *avari*, in Polish *awaria* and in Swedish *averij*. Russian has *avariya* (авария) and means wreck, crash, accident, etc.

In English, it first had the meaning of expense or loss by damage of ship or cargo, then the equitable distribution of such loss among the parties concerned. From this last meaning developed the sense of arithmetical mean which is not found in other languages.

Only the English form has the -*age* ending, and *OED* suggests that it has evidently been formed on the model of *lodemanage* (pilotage), *primage* (a payment, in addition to freight, made by shippers for loading), etc.

Eric: That was a really interesting word. Is there any other word dealing with trade and tariff?

Ahmad: As we have just been discussing a term dealing with maritime trade, I would like now to discuss a word related to dockyard. It is *arsenal*.
Eric: You are wrong. Arsenal means a collection of weapons, or a place where weapons and explosives are stored. It has nothing to do with dockyard.
Ahmad: The word originated in the dockyard. Its Arabic original is dār al-ṣinā'aħ (دارُ الصّناعَة), which, though literally means a house of manufacture, was applied to a dockyard as is evident from al-Ḥimyarī's statement in his description of Bijāyah, وبهَا دارُ صِناعَةٍ لإنْشاء الأسَاطيل لأنّ الخَشَبَ في أوْدِيَتِها وجِبَالِها كَثيرٌ, 'It has a dockyard (دارُ صِناعَة) for ship-building as there is abundant wood in its valleys and on its mountains.'[1] After giving two similar quotations from Arabic sources, Dozy says, 'C'est dans cette acception spéciale que le mot a passé dans presque toutes les langues européennes.'[2]

This Arabic word became *dársena* in Spanish and means a floating dock, inner harbour, basin. In Italian, it is *darsena* meaning dock, basin, small harbour, boat-house. With the omission of the final syllable, it became *darse* in French and

1 *Al-Rawḍ al-Miʿṭār fī Khabar al-Aqṭār*, p. 81.
2 *Op. cit.*, p. 205.

means harbour basin. There is another form in Spanish. It is *atarazana* and means, among other things, a public dockyard.

But the most well-known form of the word is *arsenal* which resulted from the omission of the initial *d*, and the addition of *-al* at the end. The omission of *d* seems to be by association with the preposition *de*, *d'* in French and some other languages.

In English, *arsenal* originally meant a dockyard as is evident from the following quotation from 1601, 'Making the Arsenall at Athens, able to receiue 1000 ships.'[1] The present meaning (a place where weapons and explosives are stored) is a natural development of the previous meaning.

This form of the word is found in most European languages. The Spanish and Portuguese *arsenal* and the Italian *arsenale* have two meanings: ammunition depot and dockyard.

But the German, Swedish, Serbo-Croatian *arsenal*, Dutch *arsenaal*, and Russian *arsenal* (арсенал) have only the first meaning.

I hope you enjoyed the exposition of this word.
Eric: Yes, I did. But it is a pity that a word like *dār al-ṣināʿah* with a constructive meaning

1 Philemon Holland, *Pliny's Historie of the World*, I. 175.

should have degenerated into a word denoting a store-house of destructive war machines.

Ahmad: You are right. We shall now discuss another word which also means a place for military stores. It is *magazine*. Its Arabic original is **makhāzin** (مَخَازِن) which is the plural of **makhzan** (مَخْزَن)[1] meaning a storehouse.

This Arabic word became *magazzino* in Italian, and means a warehouse, storehouse, shop. From Italian, it passed into French and became *magasin* meaning a store or shop. The English form *magazine* is from the French form.

The word has four important meanings. These are:

a) Warehouse or storehouse. This is the original meaning.

b) Store or shop. This meaning was developed in French.

c) The part of a gun that holds the bullets before they are fed into the breech.

d) A periodical publication like a journal.

The last two meanings were developed in English.

Here is a list of the forms and meanings of this word in different languages:

---

1 *Le Petit Robert* gives the singular as *makhzin* (with an *i*), which is wrong.

German: *Magazin*, all the meanings.

Dutch: *magazijn*, a), b) and c).

Swedish: *magasin*, a) and d).

Danish: *magasin*, all the meanings.

Serbo-Croatian: *magacin*, a) and c).

Polish: *magazyn*, a), b) and d).

Russian: *magazin* (магазин), b) and c).

Albanian: *magazinë*, a) and b).

Rumanian: *magazin* means shop, and *magazie* means storehouse. And in modern Greek, *magazi* (μαγαζι) means a shop.

Spanish and Portuguese have another form with the Arabic definite article **al-** prefixed to it. The Spanish form is *almacén* and means shop; warehouse; magazine; naval arsenal, dockyard. It has many derivatives. Here are some:

almacenar, to store, deposit.

almacenamiento, warehousing.

almacenador, warehouseman.

almacenaje, warehouse rent.

The Portuguese form is *armazém* and means a warehouse. It is to be noted here that **al-** has become **ar-** perhaps by association with *arma* meaning arm, weapon.

In both these words, the *kh*-sound of *makhzan* has been lost. In addition to this, the Portuguese word has changed the final *n* to *m*.

Eric: This was a very exhaustive and exhausting exposition.

Ahmad: Thank you. But before we leave the warehouse, I would like to point out that another derivative of this Arabic word, **al-khizānah** (الخِزَانـة) meaning storeroom, cupboard, closet, etc. has given Spanish *alacena* which also means cupboard and closet.

Eric: Shall we now leave the warehouse?

Ahmad: Yes, but as we are now in the store for weapons, ammunition and explosives, I shall very briefly touch upon a word dealing with the diameter of a projectile, or the bore of a gun.

Eric: Do you mean *calibre*?

Ahmad: Exactly. *Calibre* means the diameter of a projectile, and by extension, the internal diameter of a gun. As the calibre of a piece of ordnance determines the weight of the projectile it can throw, the word came to mean metaphorically the weight of character. It comes from the old Spanish *calibo* which is from the Arabic **qālab** (قالـب) meaning a mould. The Arabic word, however, is a borrowing from the Greek *kalapodion* (καλαποδιον) meaning a shoe last.[1]

---

1 Hoad (*OCDEE*) derives the word from the Arabic *qalaba*, to turn, but as we have seen, it is a Greek loan word. Again he writes *qālib* with an *i*. This is permissible as in *al-Miṣbāḥ al-Munīr*, but the usual vocalization is with an *a* (*qālab*).

Another form of this word is *callipers* which is an instrument for measuring the diameter of tubes or round objects.

It is to be noted that the modern Greek *kalupi* (καλουπι), and the Serbo-Croatian *kalup* both meaning mould are from the Turkish *kalıb* which is also from the same Arabic word. ... You seem to be engrossed in deep thought.

Eric: I was thinking about these strange semantic changes. Language is a powerful instrument of change: it can make and mar words, elevate or debase their meanings, turn them beautiful or ugly. In the present instance, a shoe last has come to mean character and capacity! Parodying the famous Shakespearean phrase, we may say, 'Fickleness, thy name is language!'

Ahmad: Sound thoughts beautifully expressed. Now before we say goodbye to this domain, I would like to mention here another important word dealing with trade.

Eric: Why didn't you mention it before?

Ahmad: I'm sorry, I just forgot about it.

Eric: What is the word?

Ahmad: It is *tare*.

Eric: You mean the word we use in 'tare weight'?

Ahmad: Exactly. As you know, tare is the weight of a vessel, wrapping, or container, which when subtracted from the gross weight gives the net weight. It is from the Arabic ṭarḥaḥ (طَرْحَة) meaning throwing away, subtraction. With the loss of the gutteral ḥ, the word became *tara* in Spanish, Portuguese and Italian.

French, the great trimmer of words, dropped the final *a* from the word, so it became *tare*, which is the source of the English word.

Other European languages have the Spanish-Portuguese-Italian form. German, Danish and Swedish have *tara*, and Dutch *tarra*. Russian and modern Greek also have the same form: *tara* (тара, ταρα). In Albanian, it is *tarë*. In both Russian and Albanian, it also means packing.

I shall take you now from *tare* to *tarette*.

Eric: Is it a diminutive of *tare*?

Ahmad: No, it is a huge thing; it is a merchant vessel of the Middle Ages. Lawrence Minot says,

> Eight and forty galays and mo,
> And with them als war tarettes two.[1]

It is from the Arabic ṭarīdaḥ (طريدة). It is *tarida* in modern Spanish.

Another corruption of this word is *tartan* which means a small one-masted vessel with a large lateen sail and a foresail used in the Mediterranean. William Dampier says, 'Captain

---

1 *Poems*, iii. 80 (1352).

Wright ... had taken a Spanish Tartan, wherein were 30 men, all well armed.'[1]

Spanish, Portuguese and Italian all have this word in the form of *tartana*. French as usual drops the final *a* turning the word into *tartane*.

---

1 *New Voyage Round The World* (1699).

CHAPTER 7
CLOTHING

Eric: What is the next domain we are moving into?

Ahmad: I propose to examine words dealing with clothing.

Eric: Did Arabic clothe us?

Ahmad: Yes, it did… with *cotton*.

Eric: *Cotton*! Is *cotton* Arabic?

Ahmad: Yes, it comes from the Arabic **quṭn** (قُطْن), or **quṭun**[1] (قُطُن) meaning the same.

Spanish has another form of the word with the Arabic definite article **al-** prefixed. It is *algodón* with *g* instead of *c* which is a dialectal pronunciation of the Arabic letter *qāf* (ق). This word appears in Portuguese as *algodāo*.

You probably know that French has a dislike for the phonetic combination *al*.

Eric: Does it omit it?

Ahmad: No, it changes it to *au* as you can see in

---

1 *OED* (under *acton*) has *al-qūṭun, al-qūṭn* with a long *u* in both the forms of the word, which is wrong.

the following French forms of words compared to their English forms:

palm/paume.

psalm/psaume.

balm/baume.

In accordance with this phonetic change, the Spanish *alcoton* became *aucoton* in old French. It became *acton* in English and means a stuffed jacket worn under the mail. Chaucer says,

And next his schert an aketoun,

And over that an haberjoun.[1]

In modern French, it is *haqueton*, and this form is also in use in English. Walter Scott says, 'To see the gore trickle down his rich embroidered hacqueton.'[2]

Eric: *Cotton* is probably the only word of Arabic origin dealing with clothes.

Ahmad: No, there are many more. Please wait and see.

Eric: O.K. What is your next word?

Ahmad: My next word dealing with dress material is *tabby* which means a coarse waved or watered silk. Robert Herrick says,

Let others looke for pearle and gold

---

1 *Sir Thopas*, 149.

2 *Ivanhoe*, xxviii.

Tissues or tabbies manifold.[1]

It is from the Arabic ʿattābī (عَتَّابِي) so called from al-ʿAttābiyyah (العَتَّابِيَّة), a quarter in Baghdad where the stuff was manufactured. Ibn Jubayr of Valencia who visited Baghdad in 1182 says, 'Some of the quarters [of Baghdad] are: al-ʿAttābiyyah where the ʿattābī stuff is manufactured. It is silk and cotton of diverse colours...'[2] The word became *attabi* in medieval Latin, and with the omission of the first syllable, it became *tabi* in Spanish, Portuguese and Italian. In French, it is *tabis* from which comes the English *tabby*. In Dutch, it is *tabijn* and in German, *Tabin*.

In English, *tabbinet* is a more delicate kind of tabby resembling damask used for window-curtains.[3]

As the original tabby silk was striped[4], a cat with a striped coat is called a tabby-cat. This word by extension is applied also to an old maid, and to a spiteful gossiping woman.

We will stay in Baghdad for some more time. I hope you don't mind, Eric.

---

1 *The Noble Numbers* (1647).
2 *Riḥlat ibn Jubayr*, Dār al-Kitāb al-Lubnānī, p. 162.
3 *CTCD*.
4 *OED*.

Eric: No, I don't if we are going to get another dress material.

Ahmad: Yes, another dress material connected with Baghdad is *baldachin* or *baldaquin*. It is a rich embroidered stuff, originally woven with woof of silk and warp of gold thread. The word is derived from *Baldacco*, the Italian form of *Baghdad* where it was made. Richard Hakluyt says, 'They weare Jackets ... of buckeram, scarlet, or Baldakines.'[1]

It also means a canopy placed over an altar, throne, pulpit, etc. It was so called as it originally used to be of baldachin. In the Roman Catholic Church, it is applied to the canopy borne over the priest who carries the host.

It is *baldacchino* in Italian, *baldaquín*, *baldaquino* in Spanish, *baldaquim* in Portuguese, *baldaquin* in French, *Baldachin* in German, *baldakijn* in Dutch, *baldakin* in Danish, and *baldakhin* (балдахин) in Russian, and they all mean canopy.

Eric: Baghdad has given us two words dealing with dress materials. Are there words derived from the names of other Arab cities?

Ahmad: Yes, there are. The northern Iraqi town of Mosul (المَوصِل) gave us *muslin* which is the

---

1 *Diuers Voyages Touching the Discouerie of America*, I. 54.

most delicately woven of cotton fabrics. The word is also a slang for the fair sex. William Thackeray says, 'That was a pretty bit of muslin hanging on your arm – who was she?'[1] The Scottish *muslin-kale* is a thin broth made without meat.

The Italian *mussolina* gave French its *mousseline* whence came the English *muslin*.

The word is found in most European languages. It is *muslin* in Swedish and Serbo-Croatian, *Musselin* in German and Danish, *mousseline* in Dutch, *muślin* in Polish, *muselină* in Rumanian, *museline* (μουσελινη) in modern Greek, and *muslin* (муслин) in Russian.

Eric: Are we leaving Iraq now?

Ahmad: Yes, and going to the capital of the neighbouring Syria.

Eric: That is to Damascus.

Ahmad: Yes, to Damascus which has given us *damask* and *damascene*. Let's first take the word *damask*. It is a rich silk fabric woven with elaborate designs, often of a variety of colours.[2] Lord Tennyson says, 'A damask napkin wrought with horse and hound.'[3]

---

1 *The History of Pendennis*, II. xii. 114.
2 *OED*.
3 *Audley Court*, 20.

By extension it is also applied to a twilled
linen fabric richly figured in the weaving with
designs which show up by opposite reflections of
light from the surface.[1]

It also means a variety of rose, supposed to
have been originally brought from Damascus.
Keats says, 'She ... Blush'd a live damask'.[2]

A third meaning of *damask* is steel manufactured in Damascus, and the wavy pattern on
the surface of such steel. This metal work is also
called *damascene* work. And to *damascene*
means to ornament steel with designs incised in
the surface and filled with gold or silver. Edward
Lytton says, 'His arms were damascened with
silver.'[3]

Now we go to Gaza in Palestine.

Eric: What has Gaza given us?

Ahmad: The fine *gauze* is believed to be derived
from the Arabic for *Gaza* which is **Ghazzah**
(غَزَّة). Gerhard Wahrig in his *Fremdwörter
Lexikon*, however, derives it from the Arabic
qazz (قَزّ) meaning raw silk.

Gauze is a very thin, transparent fabric of silk,
linen or cotton. Robert Browning says,

1 *OED.*
2 *Lamia*, I. 116.
3 *Harold, the Last of the Saxon Kings* (1848), III. ii.

Breast and back
Of this vivacious beauty gleamed through
gauze.[1]
Metaphorically the word also means a thin
transparent haze. Tennyson says,
Purple gauzes, golden hazes ...
Flung the torrent rainbow round.[2]
The word is found in most European
languages. It is *gaze* in Portuguese, *gasa* in
Spanish, and *gaze* in French. Italian has inserted
an *r* before the *z*, *garza*. It is *Gaze* in German
and Danish, *gaas* in Dutch, *gas* in Swedish, *gaza*
in Serbo-Croatian, Polish, and modern Greek
(γαζα), and *gaz* (газ) in Russian.
Eric: If you have finished with Gaza, I have a
question.
Ahmad: Yes, I have, and what is your question?
Eric: What about Cairo, the great seat of Arab
civilization and culture. Has it not given us any
word in this domain?
Ahmad: Well, yes and no. What I mean is that
Cairo itself has not given us any word, but one of
its precursors has. It is **al-Fusṭāṭ** (الفسطاط), which
was founded in 641 CE, and which now forms a
district of Cairo. From the name of this city came

---

1 *The Two Poets of Croisic*, 99.
2 *Vision of Sin*, ii.

the medieval Latin *(tela) fustanea* meaning the
Fustat fabric. This became *fustagno* in Italian,
fustán in Spanish, *fustão* in Portuguese, and
fustaine in old French which in modern French
has become *futaine*. From the old French form
came the English *fustian*. Formerly, it was a kind
of coarse cloth made of cotton and flax. Chaucer
says,

Of fustyan he wered a gepoun.[1]

And Shakespeare says,

The seruingmen in their new fustian.[2]

It also came to mean an unnatural bombastic
style of speaking and writing as in the
Fortnightly Review's comment, 'It was all non-
sense, and the basest kind of political fustian.'[3]
And *to fustianise* is to write fustian.

The Albanian *fustan*, the Rumanian *fustă* and
the modern Greek *fustani* (φουστανι) have all
acquired the meaning of a skirt. The modern
Greek *fustanella* (φουστανελλα) is a white kilt
worn by Greek men. The Albanian *fustan* was
adopted by the Turks in the form of *fistan* which
has become *fustān* (فُسْتَان) in modern Arabic
meaning a lady's gown.

---

1 *The Canterbury Tales: Prologue*, 75.
2 *The Taming of the Shrew*, IV. i. 49.
3 June, 1884 (838).

Eric: Is there any other Arab town which has given us a word?

Ahmad: Yes, Aleppo in Syria, which in Arabic, is Ḥalab (حَلَب). It has given us *alepine* (also spelt *alapeen*) which was a fabric made of wool and silk or mohair and cotton. John Dyer says, 'Cheyney, and baize, and serge, and alepine ... and the long countless list of woollen webs.' [1] The word is now obsolete.

In French, it is *alépine* which is the source of the English word. In Spanish, it is *alepín* which is a kind of very fine bombazine.

I have one more Arab town. Shall I mention it?

Eric: Yes, go ahead.

Ahmad: The crimson *fez* cap formerly worn by men in Turkey, Egypt and some other Middle Eastern countries is named after the ancient Moroccan town of Fez where it was originally manufactured. The Arabic name of the town is Fās (فاس). This became *Fes* in Turkish and was also applied to the cap. From Turkish, it passed into some European languages. It remained *fes* in German and Rumanian, but became *fez* in French, Dutch, Danish, Swedish and English.

It is *fesi* (φεσι) in modern Greek, *feska* (феска)

1 *Fleece* iii. 480 (1757).

in Russian, and *fetse* in Albanian.

Eric: Do you have any more Arab towns?

Ahmad: No, I don't, but I have a couple of words of Arabic origin signifying fabrics. One of them is *scarlet*.

Eric: *Scarlet* is a colour.

Ahmad: It was a fabric before it was a colour.

Eric: Will you please explain what you mean by this?

Ahmad: Of course I will. Originally *scarlet* was some rich cloth, often of a bright red colour, but also sometimes of other colours. Edmund Burke says, 'An Ambassador, whose robes are lined with a scarlet dyed in the blood of Judges.'[1]

Later it acquired the meaning of a vivid red colour. Keats says,

The poppies show their scarlet coats.[2]

And Shakespeare speaks of 'Scarlet Indignation'.[3] Scarlet fever is so called because it is accompanied by scarlet rash, and *scarlatina* is scarlet fever in a mild form.

Eric: You have not so far spoken of its Arabic origin.

Ahmad: I'll do so now. The word has a

1 *Regic. Peace*, iv. Works IX. 123.
2 *To My Brother George*, 130.
3 *Richard II*, III. iii. 99.

chequered history. The Latin *sigillatus* meaning a material with embossed figures was Arabicised in the form of **sijillāṭ** (سِجِلّاط), **siqillāṭ** (سِقِلّاط) and **siqillāṭūn** (سِقِلّاطون). A popular version of the second form was **sikirlāṭ** (سِكِرْلاّط).[1] This popular form became *scarlet(t)um* in medieval Latin, *scarlatto* in Italian, *escarlata* in Spanish and Portuguese, and *escarlate* in old French. In modern French, it is *écarlate*.

In Germanic languages, *sc-* has changed to *sh-* or *sχ-* and the final *-t* has changed to a velar sound (k, g, χ). It is *Scharlach* in German, *scharlaken* in Dutch, *scharlakan* in Swedish, and *skarlagen* in Danish.

Even languages which do not have this word use the medical term *scarlatina*. It is *skarlatina* (σκαρλατινα) in modern Greek, *skarlatina* (скарлатина) in Russian and *skarlatinë* in Albanian.

It should be noted here that the third Arabic form of the word mentioned above also passed into European languages. In English, it was *ciclatoun*, and meant a cloth of gold or other rich material, and was much esteemed in the Middle Ages. Chaucer says,

---

1 Al-Jawālīqī's *al-Muʿarrab* edited by Dr V. Abdur Rahim, 370-371, *NSOED*.

His Robe was of Syklatoun
That coste many a Jane.[1]
But the word is now obsolete.
Eric: Why do you always quote Chaucer?
Ahmad: Because he is 'the well of English undefiled' as Dryden calls him.
Eric: What's your next word?
Ahmad: My next word is *camlet*.
Eric: What is it? I have never heard this word in my life.
Ahmad: It is a kind of fabric. The *Oxford English Dictionary* says, 'A name originally applied to some beautiful and costly eastern fabric, afterwards to imitations and substitutes the nature of which has changed many times over...' It was associated with *camel* as if it is a stuff made of camel's hair. *OED* says, 'It is uncertain whether it was ever made of camel's hair; but in the 16th and 17th centuries it was made of the hair of the Angora goat.'

The word was formerly spelt with *ch*. Sir T. Herbert wrote, 'Some of rich gold or silver Chamlets, and other of cloth of gold.'[2] In Portuguese also, it is spelt with *ch*: *chamalote, chamelote*. In Spanish, it is *camelote*, and in

---

1 *Sir Thopas' Tale*, 23.
2 *A Relation of Some Yeares Travaile Bugunne Anno 1626*, 146.

Italian *cammellotto*.

It is believed to be from the Arabic **khamlaḥ**
(خَمْلَة) meaning nap, or the hairy surface of a
fabric. And from this word is derived the Arabic
mukhmal (مُخْمَل) meaning velvet.

Both *OED* and *CTCD* write this Arabic word
with a *t* (*khamlat*). This is not accurate.

Camleteen or *camletine* means an imitation
camlet.

Camlet as a verb means to variegate as a
(watered) camlet. Edmund Bolton says,
'Embroydered Gownes, Cassockes chambleted
with figures of palmes.'[1]

A coarse camlet is called *barracan*. George
Byron says, 'The striped white gauze baracan
that bound her'.[2]

It is from the Arabic **barrakān** (بَرَّكَان) which
means a cloak of camlet. It has three other
forms: *barrakānī*, *barankān*, and *barankānī*.

In Spanish, *barragán* means camlet, water-
proof woollen stuff, overcoat of such material. In
Portuguese, it is *barregana*, in Italian *baracane*,
and in French *bouracan*.

Eric: How many words pertaining to fabrics
Arabic has given us! It is very, very strange.

---

1 *The Roman Histories of Lucius Julius Florus*, I. v. 14.
2 *Don Juan*, III. lxx.

Ahmad: Please wait. More words are coming.

Eric: What more can there be?

Ahmad: There is *mohair* which is a kind of fine camlet made from the hair of the Angora goat, sometimes watered.

Eric: By the way, *mohair* is also a soldier's nickname for a civilian.

Ahmad: Exactly. It is from the Arabic **mukhayyar** (مُخَيَّر) literally meaning preferred. The form *mohair* seems to have been influenced by the English word 'hair'. From English it found its way into many languages. It is found in its English form in Dutch, Swedish and Danish. It is spelt *Mohär* in German, and *moher* in Polish. Russian has *mokher* (мохер).

But the most important is its French form. In the sense of the fabric, French retains its English form, but changed it to *moire* in the sense of watered silk. The French derived from it the verb *moirer* meaning to water the silk, and the past participle of this verb, *moiré* meaning watered silk, has spread far and wide. English, which earlier exported *mohair* to France, has now imported the French *moiré*. It is *moire* in Portuguese, *moaré* in Spanish, *moerro* in Italian, *muar* (муар) in Russian, and *Moiré* in German. German has even derived a verb from it. It is *moirieren* meaning to water.

Eric: I wonder what we Europeans wore before the Arabs gave us these beautiful fabrics.

Ahmad: Here is the name of another fabric. It is *macramé* or *macrami* meaning a fringe or trimming of knotted thread, and comes from the Turkish *makrama* which means a napkin, handkerchief, bedspread, face-towel. The Turkish word is from the Arabic **miqramah** (مِقْرَمَة) meaning a fine curtain with designs on it.

Eric: Are there any more fabrics of Arabic origin?

Ahmad: Let me think... Yes, there's *atlas*.

Eric: Atlas who bore the heavens on his shoulders?

Ahmad: No, no, I am referring to an earthly *atlas*. It is a silk-satin manufactured in the East. Thomas Baker says, 'Fat city-ladies with tawdry atlasses.'[1] It is from the Arabic **aṭlas** (أَطْلَس) meaning the same.

I just remembered another Arab town which has given us a word, but it is not in the domain of fabrics.

Eric: It doesn't matter which domain it belongs to. What is the town, and what word has it given us?

---

1 *Tunbridge Walks*, I. i.

Ahmad: It is Bijāyaḥ[1] (بجاية) in Algeria which was known for its trade in wax. The name of this town was corrupted to *bougie* in French in which it came to mean candle, and *bougie d'allumage* means spark-plug.[2]

In English also it is used in the sense of wax-candle. Maria Edgeworth says, 'Snatching up a bougie, the wick of which scattered fire behind him, he left the room.'[3]

In both French and English, *bougie* is also used as a medical term. In this sense, it means a thin flexible tube made of waxed linen introduced in the passages of the body for exploring or dilating the passages. And dilation of the passages by means of a *bougie* is called *bougienage*.

Let's go back to fabrics and clothes. Do you remember *minijupe* which some years ago was the craze in feminine sartorial fashion?

Eric: Yes, of course I do. But don't tell me that a word denoting such an outrageous dress is Arabic.

Ahmad: It is Arabic. But if the Parisian girls made three *minijupes* out of one Arabic **jubbah** (جُبَّة),

---

1 In *OED* 'بجية Bijiyah' which is wrong. *NSOED* writes it correctly.
2 From this comes بوجي for spark-plug in modern Arabic.
3 *Tales and Novels*, IX. xii. 109.

Arabic is not to be blamed.

Eric: Does *jupe* come from *jubbaĥ*?

Ahmad: Yes, it does. *Minijupe* is also called *jupette* in French. The dress in its normal size is *jupe*, which as a modern borrowing from French, means a woman's skirt. A news item in Pall Mall Gazette (10 July, 1886, 10/2) says, 'The Princess of Wales wore a corsage of white and silver brocade over a jupe of *poult de soie*.'

But formerly, it meant a loose jacket, kirtle or tunic worn by men. In Scotland it could be worn by women also.

Historically, *jupon*, which is an extension of *jupe*, was a close-fitting tunic worn under a hauberk. It also appears as *gipon*, or *gippo*. With a slightly different spelling, we have met this word in Chaucer's:

Of fustyan he wered a gepoun.[1]

Eric: Do other European languages have this word?

Ahmad: Yes, many. Spanish has the following words:

Jubón meaning doublet, jacket, waist in female dress. *Juboncito* is a diminutive of the same word, and means a small jacket or doublet. And *jubonero* is the *jubón* maker.

---

1 *Prologue*, 75.

Jubete is a doublet covered with mail. Its maker is *jubetero*, and the shop where it is sold is *jubeteria*.

Spanish also has a form with the Arabic definite article **al-** which is *aljuba*, and means Moorish garment.

Portuguese has *gibão* meaning a short jacket, or a jerkin.

Italian has *giubba* meaning a jacket, *giubettino* meaning a jumper, *giubetto* meaning a bodice, and *giubone* meaning a thick or heavy coat.

It is to be noted that unlike French, these languages have retained the original *b* of the Arabic word.

German has *Joppa* meaning a jacket. But the Dutch *jupon* meaning a petticoat is directly from French and is pronounced in the French way but without nasalization.

Russian has *yobka* (юбка) and *yobochka* (юбочка) meaning a skirt. The French *jupon* also appears as *zhupan* (жупан) which is a kind of jerkin.

We have already seen that the English forms *jupe* and *jupon* have come from French. Furthermore, we have seen that French also has *jupette* in addition to *minijupe*. I would like to add that French has a verb *juponner* meaning to put on a skirt as in *juponner une robe d'été* and *une femme bien juponnée.*

Eric: Don't you think we have spent more time with the *jupe* and *jupette* than they deserve?

Ahmad: I think it is time well spent. While tracing the history of this word through different languages, I was marvelling at how this simple Arabic word has provided Europe with sartorial devices to suit times of war and peace and luxury.

CHAPTER 8
FRUITS AND VEGETABLES

Eric: Has Arabic given us words in the domain of fruits and vegetables?

Ahmad: Oh yes. There are many words in this domain. Let me begin with *brinjal* which ultimately comes from the Sanskrit *vātingana* (वातिंगण), and became *bātingān* or *bādingān* in Persian. Arabic took it from Persian and changed it to **bādhinjān** (باذنجان) to fit it into its phonetic system. This Arabic word meaning eggplant passed into Spanish in the form of *berenjena* which became *berinjela* in Portuguese. And this was simplified to *brinjal* in English.

This word assumed another form in Spanish. Donning the Arabic definite article **al-**, it became *alberengena*. We have seen that French does not like the combination *al*, and changes it to *au*. So when *alberengena* crossed the Pyrénées and landed on French soil, it became *aubergine*.[1]

---

1 See *Le Petit Robert* and *OCDEE*, but *OED* has a different etymology which, I think, is not correct.

English and many other European languages
like German, Dutch and Swedish have borrowed
this French word.

Turkish took the Arabic *bādhinjān* and changed it to *patlıcan* and passed it on to some of the
Balkan languages. It became *patlidžan* in Serbo-
Croatian and *patëllxhan* in Albanian. Even
Russian took it from Turkish and changed it to
baklazhan (баклажан) with the substitution of *b*
for the Turkish *p*, and *k* for its *t*. The modern
Greek word *melijana* (μελιτζανα) is also from
Turkish. It has replaced the initial *p* with an *m*,
and has done away with the *t*. Italian has taken
this Greek word in the form of *melanzana*.

Rumanian also uses this Turkish-based word,
but its meaning has changed here. *Pătlăgică
roşie* (literally, blushing brinjal) means tomato,
and mostly the second word alone is used in this
context.

Eric: That was a masterly tracking of this word.
This vegetable has travelled all over the world
and has left its trace in every land it trod. ...
What's the next item on your vegetarian menu?

Ahmad: My next vegetable is *artichoke*. The
Arabic original of this word is **al-ḥaršaf** (الْحَرْشَف)
with an *ḥ*, meaning cardoon, a type of

artichoke.[1] But in later Arabic, **al-khurṡūf** (الخُرشُوف) with a *kh,* meaning artichoke, was in use.[2] This is the basis of the European forms. It became *alcarchofa* in old Spanish. Now it is *alcachofa* without the *r.* Portuguese has *alcachofra* with the *r* shunted off to the end of the word. And *alcachofral* means artichoke plantation. Portuguese uses this word in a metaphorical sense also. *Alcachofrar* means to pattern like an artichoke, to rug, to embroider with embossments. And *alcachofredo* means artichoke-patterned embroidery. The Italian *carciofo* has doffed the Arabic definite article **al-**.

As usual, French changed the word beyond recognition turning it into *artichaut* with a *t* replacing the original *f.* In English, it became *artichoke.*

Most of the other European languages have the English form slightly modified to fit into their phonetic patterns. German has *Artischocke,* Dutch has *artisjok,* Swedish has *(kron)ärtskocka,* Danish has *artiskok,* and Russian has *artishok* (артишок).

It is interesting to note that Arabic which

---

1 *Al-Ṣiḥāḥ, Tāj al-ʿArūs,* and ibn al-Bayṭār's *al-Jamiʿ li-Mufradāt al-Adwiyah wa l-Aghdhiyah,* 2:18.
2 *Muḥīṭ al-Muḥīṭ.*

provided all these European languages with the name of this vegetable has now borrowed it from one of them, and calls it *arḍī šawkī* (أرضي شوكي).[1] The most likely source of this preposterous word seems to be the German *Artischocke*.

Eric: Enough of vegetables, please. Let's now talk about fruits.

Ahmad: As you please. Do you like apricot?

Eric: Yes, I do. You seem to assign all good things to Arabic.

Ahmad: Well, these matters are decided by history and etymology. Shall I go ahead?

Eric: Yes, please.

Ahmad: The Arabic source of *apricot* is **al-barqūq**[2] (البَرقُوق) which became *albaricoque* in Spanish, *albricoque* in Portuguese. Italian dropped the *r*, and turned the word into *albicocca*.

As we have seen before, French changes *al* to *au*. This happened with this word also. In 1512 the word became *aubercot*, but later the *u* was dropped, and now it is *abricot*. Note that the final *k* sound has been replaced by *t,* and even this letter is only for show: it is not pronounced.

When this distorted French form of the word

---

1 This is in the Lebanese dialect.

2 Now it means plum in Egyptian Arabic.

entered English, it underwent another change. Its *b* was changed to *p*, thus changing the word to *apricot*.

Eric: Why was the *b* changed to *p*?

Ahmad: Due to false etymology. The word was thought to be from the Latin *in aprico coctus* meaning ripened in a place exposed to the sun.

Other European languages have the English form with another change. The final *t* has been changed to *s*! German has *Aprikose*, Dutch *abrikoos*, Swedish *aprikos*, Danish *abrikos*, and Russian *abrikos* (абрикос).

Languages like Serbo-Croatian, Macedonian, Rumanian and Albanian have not borrowed this Arabic word. They use the Turkish word *kayısı* instead.

Eric: It was a pretty long exposition. Do you have anything else to say about *apricot*?

Ahmad: Yes, there is one more point I have to tell you about. The Arabic *al-barqūq* is originally a Latin word which the Arabs borrowed from the Greeks. The Latin *praecoquum* or *praecox* meaning early ripe was an epithet of this fruit which was originally called *prunum*. This word became *praikokion* (πραικοκιον) in Greek, and this is the word which entered Arabic in the form of *barqūq*. And we have already seen its later history.

Eric: Do you have any other fruit?

Ahmad: Yes, the luscious *orange*.

Eric: I thought it is somehow connected to the Latin *aurum* meaning gold.

Ahmad: That is what people thought, but it is not. It is ultimately from the Persian *nārang* (نارنگ) which Arabic borrowed, and to suit its phonetic system, changed it to **nāranj** (نارنج). This Arabic word became *naranja* in Spanish. It has many derivatives:

naranjada, orangeade.

naranjado, orange-coloured.

naranjal, orange-grove.

naranjero, orange-seller.

Like many other Arabic words, this word also entered in two forms: one without the definite article, and the other with the definite article attached. We see the second form in *anaranjado* (orange-coloured) which is another form of *naranjado*.

In Portuguese, the initial *n* has been changed to *l*, so the word has become *laranja*.

When the word crossed the Pyrénées and arrived in France, two very important changes took place in the word. First, the initial *n* was completely lost. Secondly, the *a* was changed to *o*. After these two changes, the word became *orange*.

Eric: It is very strange. Why did this happen?

Ahmad: For two reasons. The *n* was lost due to confusion between it and the *n* of the article *une*. And the change of *a* to *o* seems to be due to our old friend, folk etymology. The word was presumed to be connected with the French *or* meaning gold. The bright yellow colour of the fruit must have strengthened this supposition. After these cosmetic operations, *naranj* became *orange*.

Eric: I am afraid that one day we might say *an apkin* instead of *a napkin*.

Ahmad: We may or we may not. But there are words which have actually undergone this kind of change. A *nickname* was originally *an eke-name* where *eke* means addition as in *to eke out a living*. Another interesting example is *an umpire* which originally was *a nonpeer* meaning not equal. Would you like to have one more example?

Eric: Yes, please. It is such an interesting subject.

Ahmad: The tailed amphibian *newt* was originally *an ewt*. The original *ewt* now survives in *eft* which is a kind of lizard. Charles Churchill says,

In quest of food,

Efts strove in vain to crawl.[1]

Eric: How interesting! Let's go back to our *orange*. Anything more about this interesting word?

Ahmad: Yes. Italian also dropped the initial *n*, but did not tamper with the *a*. With a little cosmetic change to the termination, it changed the Arabic *nāranj* to *arancia*. This word has many derivatives. These are:

aranceto, orange plantation.

aranciata, orangeade.

aranciato, orange-coloured.

aranciera, orangery.

arancio, orange tree.

arancione, orange (colour).

There is another word in Italian for orange: it is *melarancia*. It is the same *arancia* with *mela* meaning *apple* prefixed to it.

Eric: Our *orange* is obviously from French.

Ahmad: Yes. English adopted this amputated form of the word from French. Some other languages also have this French-English form. German has *Orange*, and Dutch *oranje*.

There is another interesting point. We have seen earlier that the Italian word for orange is *arancia*. Italian also has *ranciato* (without the

---

1 *Poems*, I. 112.

initial *a)* meaning orange-coloured. This word pops up in German and Dutch. In German, *Pomeranze* means bitter orange. In Dutch and Swedish, it is *pomerans*. The first part of this compound word, *pome*, is the Latin *pomum* meaning fruit which has become *pomme* in French meaning apple.

I have now finished with orange.

Eric: Don't you want to give us another fruit?

Ahmad: Certainly. How about *tangerine*? I could have mentioned this earlier when I was dealing with words derived from the names of Arab towns and cities. Tangerine, whose botanical name is *Citrus nobilis*, comes from Tanger or Tangier, the seaport in Morocco, on the Strait of Gibraltar. Its Arabic name is Ṭanjah (طَنجَة) about which the Arab poet Baššār ibn Burd says,

وَطَنْجَةُ ذاتُ العَجَبِ

'And Tangier, the city of wonders.'

I must mention here in passing that *Gibraltar* is also an Arabic word. It is a corruption of its Arabic name **Jabal Ṭāriq** (جَبَلُ طارق), the Mount of Ṭāriq, named after Ṭāriq ibn Ziyād, who landed there at the beginning of the Arab conquest of Spain. In English, it has come to mean an impregnable stronghold. Ralph Emerson says, 'In this Gibraltar of propriety, mediocrity gets intrenched, and consolidated.'[1]

Gibraltar is also a kind of sweetmeat.

Eric: Perhaps we can close our discussion on vegetables and fruits with the mention of this sweetmeat.

Ahmad: O.K. But after we study *Musa*.

Eric: Who is *Musa*? And what does he have to do with our study?

Ahmad: *Musa* is not a man. It is a fruit.

Eric: I haven't heard of a fruit by this name.

Ahmad: Yes, you are right. But it is the botanical name of the banana and the tropical plantain, and the family is called *Musaceae*. Formerly, the banana was also called the *muse*. Henry Lyte says, 'Of Musa or Mose tree ... The Mose tree leaues be so great and large, that one may easyly wrap a childe ... in them.'[2]

It is from the Arabic **mawz** (مَوْز) meaning bananas. It is a collective noun, and the singular is *mawzah*.

There is another fruit, but it is used as livestock feed. Shall I tell you about it?

Eric: Yes, I would like to know.

Ahmad: It is *carob*. It is from the Arabic **kharrūb**

---

1 *English Traits, Manners, Works* (Bohn), II. 50.
2 *Dodoens' Niewe Herball or Historie of Plantes*, tr. 1578, VI. xxxviii. 704.

(خَرُّوب) which became *carrubia* in medieval Latin whence come the Italian *carruba* and the French *caroube*, and this French form is the source of the English word.

Spanish took this word with the Arabic article prefixed to it, but changed the *kh* to *g*. The result is *algarroba*. Even English has borrowed this form from Spanish. Robert Bentley says, 'The legumes of *Prosopis dulcis* ... are used as a food for cattle, under the name of Algorobo.'[1]

Eric: Doesn't Portuguese have this word?

Ahmad: Yes, it has this same form with **al-**, but it has changed the *kh* to *f*. So the Portuguese word is *alfarroba*. Strange, isn't it?

Eric: Yes, very strange.

Ahmad: Here is another very interesting fact about this word. Carob is also called locust-bean or St. John's Bread because it is generally identified with the locust eaten by John the Baptist. In German, it is called *Johannisbrot*, i.e. John's bread.

---

1 *A Manual of Botany* (1887), p. 504.

CHAPTER 9
SEASONINGS

Eric: I assume you are now finished with vegetables and fruits.

Ahmad: Yes. If you like, we will now study a seasoning that is used in cooking to give colour and flavour to food.

Eric: What is it?

Ahmad: It is *saffron*.

Eric: That must be interesting.

Ahmad: Let's see. In addition to its flavour, *saffron* is also used to denote its bright orange-yellow colour. Chaucer says,

His heer, his berd was lyk saffroun.[1]

Shakespeare says,

I must haue Saffron to colour the Warden Pies.[2]

The Arabic source of *saffron* is **zaʻfarān** (زَعْفَران) meaning the same. The word has two

---

1 *Sir Thopas*, 19.
2 *The Winter's Tale*, IV. iii. 48.

forms in European languages: one with the Arabic definite article **al-**, and the other without it. From the first form comes the Spanish *azafrán*. The following derivatives are used in Spanish:

azafranar, to dye with saffron.

azafranado, saffron-coloured.

azafranamiento, saffron-dying.

azafranal, saffron plantation.

azafranero, saffron dealer.

From the same form comes the Portuguese *açafrão* which also has many derivatives.

The second form is represented by the Italian *zafferano*, and the French *safran*. The English *saffron* comes from the French form.

Most of the other European languages have adopted the French form. German and Danish have *safran*, Dutch *saffraan*, and Swedish *saffran*.

Slavic languages have *sh* instead of *s*. In Russian and Macedonian, it is *shafran* (шафран). Even Rumanian and Albanian show this trait. The first has *şofran*, and the latter *shafran*.

Eric: Please tell me what is *bastard saffron*?

Ahmad: I am glad you asked me that question. But how did you know this word?

Eric: I read in a book on cosmetics that rouge is made from the dyestuff obtained from the florets of this plant.

Ahmad: Exactly.

Eric: Why is it called *bastard saffron*?

Ahmad: The real name of this plant is *safflower*. Its botanical name is *Carthamus tinctorius*. It is wholly different from saffron, but it was often used as a substitute for saffron in medicine, and that is why it was given this strange name.

Eric: Is it also an Arabic word?

Ahmad: Yes. Its Arabic name is 'uṣfur[1] (عُصْفُر). It became *alazor* in Spanish and *açafroa* in Portuguese. The *al* or *a* at the beginning of these words is the Arabic definite article. The form without **al-** is represented by the old French *saffleur*, and the German *Safflor*. These forms have been influenced by association with *saffron* and *flower*.

Eric: Let's go back to *saffron*.

Ahmad: I have finished with *saffron* both real and bastard.

Eric: Any other seasoning?

Ahmad: Yes, but this seasoning is used to flavour soups and salads.

Eric: What is it?

Ahmad: It is *tarragon*. Its botanical name is *Artemisia Dracunculus*. Its Arabic source is

---

1 *NSOED* has *aṣfar*, which is wrong.

ṭarkhūn (طَرْخُون) meaning the same, which, according to some scholars, is from the Greek *drakon*
(δρακων).
It has three forms in European languages:
1. like the English form: Spanish has
   tarragón, and Italian *targone*.
2. with *est-* at the beginning: Portuguese has
   estragão, and French and German
   estragon. In addition to *tarragón*, Spanish
   also has *estragón*. In Russian, it is *estragon*
   (естрагон).
3. with *dr-* instead of *tarr-*: Dutch and
   Swedish have *dragon*. Danish has a combination of forms 2 and 3: *esdragon*.
Eric: Do you have any other seasoning products?
Ahmad: No, no more seasonings. But I would
like to tell you about a flavouring.
Eric: Flavouring?
Ahmad: Yes. The *lemon*. This word is from the
Arabic **laymūn** (لَيْمُون)[1] which itself is a loan word
from Persian where it is *līmū* (لِيمُو), but ultimately
it is from Sanskrit.
   It is *limón* in Spanish, *limão* in Portuguese,
limone in Italian and *limon* in French. This
French form is the source of the English *lemon*.
It is to be noted that English has *e* after *l* while

---

1 *OCDEE.*

the other languages have *i*.

Some East European languages also use this word. Albanian has *limon*, Serbo-Croatian has *limun*, Russian and Macedonian have *limon* (лимон). And it is *lemonion* (λεμονιον) in modern Greek.

The French *limon* does not mean lemon; it means lime which is a kind of lemon. French uses *citron* for lemon. And so do the Germanic languages. But whether they use *lemon* or not, they all use *lemonade*.

The word *lime* is also from the same Arabic source. Spanish and Portuguese also have it in the form of *lima*.

Eric: The very name of lemonade has invigorated me.

Ahmad: That is good. We can carry on our discussion with renewed strength.

Eric: We have seen seasoning and flavouring. What else do you have?

Ahmad: I have a vegetable product which is used in cookery as a relish.

Eric: What is it?

Ahmad: It is *tamarind*. In Arabic, it is called **tamr hindī** (تَمْر هِنْدِيّ), i.e. Indian date. This word became *tamarindo* in Spanish, Portuguese and Italian. The original form seems to have been *tamarindi* which in Italian is the plural form[1], and it was made singular by changing it to *tamarindo*.[2]

As we have seen, French is a trimmer of words. It has dropped the final *d* from the word and made it *tamarin* although in old French it was *tamarandi*.

In German, Dutch and Danish, it is *tamarinde*, and in Swedish, *tamarind[frukt]*. Russian has *tamarind* (тамаринд).

I want to round off the discussion of words dealing with seasoning, flavouring and relish with a word meaning pickle, but it is not used in English.

Eric: In which language is it used?

Ahmad: In Spanish and Portuguese. The word in both these languages is *escabeche*. In Spanish, it means pickle, pickled fish, souse. The verb *escabechar* not only means to pickle, but also to stab and kill!

In Portuguese, *escabeche* has the additional meaning of disguise.

The source of this word is the Arabic **al-sikbāj**

---

1 As *paparazzi*, the plural of *paparazzo*.
2 Cf. the English word *pea* which was originally *pease* but was mistaken for a plural, and the *s* was dropped to form the new singular *pea*.

(السِّكْبَاج) which is a dish of meat cooked with vinegar. It is a Persian loan word in Arabic. In modern Persian, it is *sikbā* (سکبا), and is made up of *sirka*, vinegar and *bā*, dish. But it was *sikpāg* in Pehlevi which is the Persian prevalent during the 6th century CE.

CHAPTER 10
SWEETS

Eric: Has Arabic given us anything in the field of cookies, cakes, etc.?

Ahmad: Can there be cookies and cakes without sugar?

Eric: Do you mean to say that *sugar* is Arabic?

Ahmad: Yes, that's what I mean.

Eric: But sugar is one of the basic necessities of life, and we should have had it before we got it from the Arabs. What did we sweeten our cakes with before that?

Ahmad: I don't know that, but I know for sure that *sugar* is Arabic.

Eric: O.K. Please tell me about it.

Ahmad: The Arabic word for sugar is **sukkar** (سُكَّر) which is from *šakar* (شَکَر) in Persian. Like some other Arabic words, this word also entered European languages in two forms: one without the definite article **al-**, and another with the article attached.

Now, the first form became *succarum* in

medieval Latin whence comes the Italian *zucchero*, and the French *sucre*.

From the other form, *al-sukkar* (which is pronounced *as-sukkar*) come the Spanish *azúcar*, and the Portuguese *açúcar*.

Most of the other European languages have the first form. German has *Zucher*, Dutch *suiker*, Danish *sukker*, Swedish *socker*, and Polish *cukier*.

In a few languages like Russian and modern Greek, the *k* has been changed to *kh*. In the former it is *sakhar* (caxap), and in the latter, *zakharis* (ζαχαρις). Rumanian has *zahar* where the guttural *kh* has been changed to *h*.

Some East European languages with close ties with Turkey have adopted the Turkish form of the word *şeker* (pronounced *sheker*). But in these languages, the *k* has been palatalized to *ch*. So Albanian has *sheqer* (pronounced *shecher*), and Macedonian has *shecher* (шекеp). Serbo-Croatian has both *cukar* (in the west) and *šećer* (in the east).

Eric: Any other sweet word?

Ahmad: Yes, *candy*. Like *sugar*, this word comes ultimately from the Sanskrit *khandah* (खंड:). It became *kand* (كند) in Persian whence came the Arabic **qand** (قند). Its adjectival form **qandī** (قندي) gave the European languages *candy*. In French, it became *sucre candi*, and it was taken to be a past participle, so the verb *candir* was formed. Italian also created the verb *candire* meaning to candy, and its past participle is *candito* as in *frutto candito*, crystallized fruit. Portuguese has *cande* as in *açúcar-cande*. It also has *candil*, and the verb is *candilar* meaning to candy, to coat with sugar, to crystallize, to conserve by boiling with sugar.

In German, *Kandi* does not stand alone, but as a compound with *Zucker* (*Kandizucker*). The verb is *kandieren*, to candy, and the past participle is *kandiert*. In Swedish, it is used as a compound with *socker* (*kandisocker*). In Danish, it is *kandis*, and the verb is *kandisere*.

Unlike other languages, English has many meanings of the verb to *candy*, one of them is to cover something with a crystalline substance, as hoar-frost. Shakespeare says,

The cold Brooke Candied with ice.[1]

William Browne says,

Hoary frosts had candy'd all the plaines.[2]

---

1 *Timon of Athens*, IV. iii. 226.
2 *Britannia's Pastorals*, I. iv. (1972) I. 119.

CHAPTER 11
DRINKS

Eric: Any other sweet word, Ahmad?
Ahmad: No. Let's now study some words denoting drinks. We have already seen *coffee, mocha* and *lemonade.* My next word is *syrup.* As you know, it is a thick sweet liquid, especially medicated or as a vehicle of medicine. Shakespeare says,

> Not Poppy, nor Mandragora,
> Nor all the drowsie Syrrups of the world.[1]

Keats says,

> Lucent syrops, tinct with cinnamon.[2]

The word is from the Arabic **šarāb**[3] (شَرَاب) meaning a drink. It is derived from the verb *šariba,* to drink. This word became *siropus* in medieval Latin whence it entered other European languages.

In Italian, it became *sciroppo* or *siroppo.* The verb *sciroppare* means to preserve in syrup, or to

---

1 *Othello,* III. iii. 331.
2 *The Eve of St. Agnes,* xxx.
3 *Le Petit Robert* has *sarab* with an *s,* which is wrong. *Sarāb* in Arabic means mirage.

sweeten.

In Portuguese, it is *xarope*. It should be noted here that in Portuguese and old Spanish, the letter *x* stands for the sound of *sh* as in *she*. In this connection, I should mention that it has been suggested that the use of *x* in algebra for the unknown number reflects the Arabic use of ش (š) which stands for **šay³** (شَيْءٌ) meaning *something*.

Now back to *xarope*. This word not only signifies syrup, but also means home-made remedy or purgative, and in Brazilian popular use, a tiresome thing. This last meaning seems to have developed from the meaning of purgative. *Xaropada* means cough syrup. The verb *xaropar* means to treat (someone) with syrup. There is another verb, *enxaropar* which means to give syrup as a remedy. And *enxaropar se* means to get drunk.

Spanish has two forms of this word: *jarabe* and *jarope*.

Eric: Why are they written with *j*?

Ahmad: As I mentioned before, in old Spanish, *x* was pronounced *sh*. In modern Spanish, this sound has undergone a change. It is now pronounced like the Arabic خ, or the German *ch* in *Buch*. And it is represented by the letter *j*. So a Spaniard would say, 'I am going to San Khose in Khunio, and coming back in Khulio' (I am going to San Jose in June and coming back in July).[1]

Eric: That is very interesting.

Ahmad: Let's go back to *jarabe*. It means syrup. And the verb *jarabear* means to prescribe syrups very often, and to take syrup frequently.

French has *sirop*. The verb *siroter* (with a *t* replacing the *p*!) means to sip, e.g. *siroter son café*.

In many other European languages, the English form of the word has been adopted with slight modifications. It is *Sirup* in German, Danish and Serbo-Croatian, *siroop* in Dutch, *sirap* in Swedish, *syrop* in Polish and Rumanian, and *shurup* in Albanian. Modern Greek has *siropi, siropion* (σιροπι, σιροπιον), Russian *sirop* (сироп), and Macedonian *sirup* (сируп).

Eric: The 'drowsy syrup' is making me really drowsy. Shall we move on to some other word?

Ahmad: Please tarry a while. There are four variants of this word which I would like you to know. First, I'll tell you about *shrub* which is a drink of lemon or orange juice with rum or other spirit. Dickens says, 'Miss Ivins's friend's

---

1 Cf. *junta* which in the USA is pronounced *hunta*.

young man would have the ladies go into the Crown, to taste some shrub.'[1] This word comes from the Arabic **šarāb** also, but through Urdu where it means wine or spirits.

The second word is *shrab* which is used in an Anglo-Indian context and means wine, spirits or a drink prepared with them. It also comes from the same Arabic word.

The third word is *sherbet* which is from the Turkish *şerbet* from **šarbaħ** (شَرْبَة), another word for drink in Arabic. It is a fruit-juice cooling drink. Byron says,

> A cup too on the board was set
> That did not seem to hold sherbet.[2]

The fourth word is *sorbet* which, in addition to meaning *sherbet* also means a kind of frozen sweetmeat made from sugar and fruit juice. Hence *sorbetière* means a domestic ice-cream-making machine. This is also from the same Turkish form of the Arabic *šarbaħ*, but entered Europe via Italy.

Eric: This Arabic *šarbaħ* seems to be a prolific multiplier.

Ahmad: Yes, and also a great globe-trotter. It

1 *Sketches by Boz, Miss Evans and the Eagle.*
2 *The Bride of Abydos,* II. viii.

has made three journeys to Europe: first, directly, second, via India and third, via Turkey. In Italian, it became *sorbetto*, and has the same two meanings as in English. It has many derivatives, but most of them relate to ice-cream only. These are:

sorbettare, to freeze ice-cream.

sorbettiera, ice-box.

sorbettiere, ice-cream seller.

The French *sorbet*, which is the immediate source of the English word, also means sherbet and ice-cream, and unlike English, in French, *sorbetière* means utensils and appliances for making both sherbet and ice-cream.

In Portuguese, it is *sorvete*, and has broadly the same two meanings. Here also the derivatives are related to ice-cream only. *Sorveteira* means ice-cream freezer, *sorveteiro*, ice-cream vendor, and *sorveteria*, ice-cream shop.

The Spanish *sorbete* means sherbet, but *sorbetera* means ice-cream freezer.

Eric: Is it found in other European languages?

Ahmad: Yes, German, Dutch, Danish and Swedish have the English form of the word, i.e. *sorbet*.

Eric: What next?

Ahmad: After *syrup*, it is but natural to mention

julep.

Eric: And what is this *julep*?

Ahmad: Well, it is a sweet drink used as a vehicle for medicine. It is sometimes medicated and used as a demulcent, or gently stimulating mixture. Joseph Hall says,

> The wholesome julap, whose receat
> Might his diseases lingring force defeat.[1]

Referring to its soothing quality, William Chamberlayne says,

> Whose heat, not all
> The jewleps of their tears (could quench).[2]

But in the USA, *julep* is different. It is a mixture of brandy, whiskey, or other spirit with sugar and ice and some flavouring, usually mint.[3] Cornwallis says, 'San Francisco was all bustle and illumination, with glittering bars filled with julep-drinkers.'[4]

The Arabic source of this word is **julāb** (جُلاب) which literally means rose-water. It is a loan word from Persian where it is *gulāb* (گلاب) from *gul*, rose and *āb*, water. This Arabic word became *julapium* in medieval Latin. In Spanish, it is *julepe*, and in Portuguese, *julepo*.

---

1 *Satan's Fiery Darts Quenched* (1647), II. iv. 27.
2 *Pharonnida: a heroick poem* (1659).
3 *OED*.
4 *New World*, I. 76.

In Italian, it is *giulebbe*, and the verb *giulebbare* means to stew fruit, to sweeten, to render (a food) palatable. Another extended colloquial verb, *giulebbarsi* means to swallow, to put up with, to cherish, to sweeten.

In French, it is *julep* which is the immediate source of the English form.

As both *syrup* and *julep* have medicinal uses, I shall now tell you of a shrub with medicinal qualities.

Eric: Of course of Arabic origin.

Ahmad: Yes, of course. It is *senna*. It is a shrub bearing yellow flowers. John Scott says,

In vain the senna waves its glossy gold.[1]

Its dried leaflets are used as a purgative. Its Arabic is **sanā**[2] (سَنَا), meaning the same, which appears as *sena* in Spanish and Portuguese, and *senna* in Italian. French has *séné*.

In Germanic languages, the word is rarely used alone: the word for *leaves* is mostly suffixed to it. It is **Sennesblätter** in German, **senebladeren** in Dutch, **sennablad** in Swedish, and **sennesblade** in Danish.

Even modern Greek has this word where it is *sena* (σενα).

---

1 *Poetical Works* (1782), 261.
2 *Le Petit Robert* has *sanas* (with an *s* at the end), which is wrong.

CHAPTER 12
SCIENCE

Eric: No more of this purgative, please. Let's change the subject. At the beginning of our talk, you mentioned some words pertaining to science. Can you mention some more if there are any?

Ahmad: Yes, of course. How about *benzene*?

Eric: *Benzene* is Arabic? Are you kidding?

Ahmad: No, I am not. I'll tell you its history. It is indeed very interesting. Originally the Arabic word had nothing to do with science. It was a word dealing with a kind of perfume. The Arabic word is **lubān jāwī** (لبان جاوي), i.e. frankincense of Java. It is the aromatic and resinous juice of Styrax, a tree of Java and Sumatra, used in perfumery. In this sense, the Arabic word became *benjui* in Spanish, *benjoim* in Portuguese, *benzoino* in Italian, and *benjoin* in French. These Romance languages seem to have dropped the initial *lu,* confusing it with the article.

The English form is from the French. The English first took the French word *benjoin*, but later changed it to *benzoin*. Later on it was further corrupted to *benjamin*. The poet, Robert Herrick, says,

> Leave a name as sweet
> As Benjamin or Storax when they meet.[1]

The word *benzoin* is also applied to a chemical called bitter-almond-oil camphor which is one of the constituents of gum-benzoin.

From *benzoin* was formed in 1800 the chemical term *benzoic* acid, whence later on were formed *benzol*, *benzine*, and other terms of the *benzene* series.

Eric: That is really a very interesting word. Have you got any other words dealing with chemistry?

Ahmad: Yes. My next word is *alkali*.

Eric: I never thought that *alkali* can be Arabic, but it has an Arabic look.

Ahmad: Yes, because of the initial *al*. Its Arabic is al-qalīy (القلي) which literally means fried or roasted from *qalā*[2], to fry, roast in a pan. As a

---

1 *Hesperides* (1869), 139.
2 *OED* has *qalay*, which is wrong. The original form of the verb, of course, is *qalaya* which, according to Arabic phonetic rules, becomes *qalā*.

medical term, it is applied to the calcined ashes of Salsola and Salicornia plants.

Before it acquired the present-day chemical connotation, *alkali* meant soda-ash. It also meant the Salsola plant which is the source of the Arabic alkali. Lyte says, 'It [Salsola Kali] is the right Kali or Alkali of the Arabians: some call it in English Salte-worte; we may also call it Kali or prickled Kali.'[1]

It goes without saying that *alkali* as a chemical term is found in all the languages.

Eric: That is also interesting. Many of us do not know that the speakers of Arabic had anything to do with the development of science.

Ahmad: Language is a faithful record of human civilization.

Eric: Please go ahead with your next word.

Ahmad: My next word is *talc*, a very soft and pliable mineral.

Eric: From which is prepared the *talcum* powder used in skin care.

Ahmad: Exactly. It is from the Arabic ṭalq[2] (طلق) meaning the same. It became *talcum* in medieval Latin. It is *talco* in Spanish, Portuguese and Ital-

---

1 *Dodoens' Niewe Herball*, 115.
2 Ibn al-Bayṭār, *op. cit.*, p. 3:103.

ian. French as usual chopped off the final *o*, so the word became *talc* which is the source of the English word.

Other languages mostly have the English form of the word. In German, Dutch, Danish and Swedish, it is written with a *k* (*talk*). In German, talcum powder is *Talkpuder*, in Dutch *talk-poeder*. In Danish, *talk* is talc, and *talkum* is talcum powder.

In Russian, *tal'k* (тальк) means both talc and talcum powder. In modern Greek, it is *talkes* (ταλκης).

Eric: If you have finished with *talcum powder*, let's go on to the next word.

Ahmad: O.K. My next word is another mineral. It is *borax*. It is hydrated sodium tetraborate, found on alkaline lakeshores. Chaucer says,

> Ther nas quyksilver, litarge, ne brimstone,
> Boras, ceruce, no oille of tartre noon.[1]

The Arabic word is **būraq**[2] (بُورق) meaning the same. It became *borax* in medieval Latin. It is *bórax* in Spanish and Portuguese, *borax* in French, and *borace* in Italian.

Almost all other European languages have the English form of the word. Russian has *bura*

---

1 *Prologue*, 630.
2 *Tāj al-ʿArūs*.

(бура).

Eric: Is the word *baroque* related to *borax*?

Ahmad: Yes and no. They are etymologically related to each other in Arabic, but not in English and other European languages. In Portuguese, *barroca* means a gutter made by a water-flood, uneven stony ground. This is believed by etymologists to be from the Arabic **buraq**[1] (بُرَق), plural of *burqah* (بُرْقـة) meaning a rough stony ground. Portuguese has another word, *barroco* which means a rough or imperfect pearl. In this sense, Spanish has *barrueco*. From the irregular shape of the pearl developed meanings like whimsical, grotesque, odd. In Italian, *barroco* means odd, awkward, in bad taste.

It was also applied to a bold, vigorous, exuberant style in architecture.

Eric: Let's now go back to our chemical terms.

Ahmad: O.K. A metallic substance bearing an Arabic name is *antimony*, but its metallic characteristics are less pronounced than those of the metals generally. It is from the medieval Latin *antimonium* which is believed by scholars to be a corruption of the Arabic **ithmid** (إثْمِد) meaning the same.

---

1 *OED* and *CTCD*.

Eric: Is there any other chemical substance bearing an Arabic name?

Ahmad: Yes. There is *natron* which is the native sesquicarbonate of soda. It has another form, *anatron* where *a* represents the Arabic article **al-**. It is from the Arabic **al-naṭrūn** (النَّطْرُون) meaning the same, which itself is from the Greek *nitron* (νιτρον).

The immediate source of the English word is the French *natron*. It is *natrón* in Spanish and *natrão* in Portuguese. The word is used in many other European languages. In Russian, it is *natr* (натр).

It must be mentioned here that *natrium*, another name of sodium, is from this word. The chemical symbol of sodium, *Na*, refers to this word. *Natro-* is used to form the names of minerals containing sodium as a primary constituent, or as a constituent atom, as *natroalunite*.

Eric: Any other chemical name?

Ahmad: Yes, there are many more. A mineral bearing an Arabic name is *realgar* which is arsenic monosulphide. Its Arabic name is **rahj al-ghar**[1] (رَهْجُ الغَار) literally meaning the powder of the cave. The word *rahj* meaning powder is applied

---

1 Ibn al-Bayṭār, *op. cit.*, p. 3:67 under the word شك , and Dozy, *op. cit.*, pp. 332-333.

to arsenic.

The word became *realgar* in medieval Latin. As can be seen, the letters *h* and *j* were lost in the Latin form.

It is *rejalgar* in Spanish. Portuguese has two forms: *realgar* and *rosalgar*. In French, it is *réalgar*. German has the same form as the English. Russian has *real'gar* (реальгар).

Now, this 'powder of the cave' reminds me of another powder. You may call it the 'powder of the eye.'

Eric: What is it?

Ahmad: I mean *alcohol*.

Eric: But alcohol is not a powder.

Ahmad: It was a powder, but now it is a liquid. Language can liquefy a powder, and solidify a liquid.

Eric: You have aroused my curiosity. Please explain. I am all ears.

Ahmad: The Arabic source of *alcohol* is **al-kuḥl** (الْكُحْل) which is the fine powder used to stain the eyelids. Originally this is what the word *alcohol* meant. George Sandys says, 'They put betweene the eye-lids and the eye a certaine black powder ... made of a minerall brought from the kingdome of Fez, and called Alcohole.'[1]

---

1 *A Relation of a Journey Begun 1610* (Travels) 1615.

Here is how this powder turned into a liquid:

o First, by extension it was applied to any fine impalpable powder produced by sublimation as *alcohol of sulphur* for the flower of brimstone. *Physics Dictionary* (1657) defines *alcolismus* as 'an operation ... which reduceth a matter into allcool, the finest pouder that is.'

o Secondly, by further extension of this idea of sublimation to liquids, it was applied to an essence or spirit obtained by distillation or 'rectification', as *alcohol of wine*, i.e. essence or spirit of wine. Edward Phillips writes in *The New World of English Words* (1706), '*Alcohol* or *Alcool*, the pure Substance of anything separated from the more Gross. It is more especially taken for a most subtil and highly refined Powder, and sometimes for a very pure Spirit: Thus the highest rectified Spirit of Wine is called *Alcohol Vini.*' Metaphorically, it was applied to the quintessence of anything. Samuel Coleridge says, 'Intense selfishness, the alcohol of egotism.'[1]

o Thirdly, *alcohol of wine* was shortened to

---

1 *Lectures and Notes on Shakespeare and Other English Poets* (1834), II. 117.

simply *alcohol* as it was the most familiar of rectified spirits.

Eric: What an interesting history, or shall I call it a story? It is now clear that words are not born with their meanings inscribed on their foreheads. They are in constant change, i.e. their forms, their sounds and their meanings.

Ahmad: That is the truth.

Eric: You said language can liquefy powders, and solidify liquids. We have just seen an instance of the first. Do you have an example of the second?

Ahmad: Yes. We have just seen that *sorbet* which is essentially a drink has also come to mean a frozen sweetmeat made from sugar and fruit juice.

I would like to draw your attention to a very important fact. Some of the meanings of *alcohol* which are obsolete in English, and have only historical significance, are alive in Spanish. *Alcohol* in Spanish has the following meanings: alcohol, spirit of wine, antimony, galena, cosmetic used for eyebrows.

The verb *alcoholar* has the following meanings: to distil alcohol from, to dye or paint with antimony, (*naut.*) to tar after caulking, to pulverize.

And its past participle, *alcoholado*, besides

meaning *alcoholized*, also means *of a darker colour round the eyes* (cattle).

The original meaning of *al-kuḥl* is retained in the English *kohl*. Thomas Moore says,

> Others mix the Kohol's jetty die
> To give that long, dark languish to the eye.[1]

French has *khôl* in this sense. It has two other forms: *kohol* and *koheul*. Albert Cossery says, 'Ses yeux exagérément noircis au khôl.'[2]

Eric: So the original meaning of antimony lingers on.

Ahmad: Yes, very much so. I have to tell you now the different forms of this word in the various languages of Europe. There are two basic forms: one with *h*, and the other without it.

Most languages have retained the *h* of the original Arabic. Apart from English, Spanish and Dutch have *alcohol* (with *c*). German, Swedish, Danish, Polish and Serbo-Croatian have *alkohol* (with *k*).

French, Portuguese, Italian, Rumanian and Albanian have *alcool*.[3] Modern Greek also has it without the *h*: *alkool* (αλκοολ).

---

1 *Lalla Rookh, Veiled Prophet* (1817), II.
2 *Le Petit Robert*.
3 Albanian writes it with a *k*.

Russian has changed its *h* to *g*. The Russian form of the word is *alkogol'* (алкоголь). Macedonian has changed it to *kh*. It has *alkokhol* (алкохол).

Eric: Any more chemical terms?

Ahmad: Yes, there is a chemical, which like alcohol, has to do with the treatment of the eye. It is *tutty* which chemically is crude zinc oxide. Humphrey Lloyd says, 'Tuty doth dry and clear the eyes, more than any medycynes.'[1]

It is from the Arabic **tūtiyā'** (تُوتِيَاء) from *tūtiyā* in Persian, but ultimately from the Sanskrit *tūtaka* (तूतक).

The Arabic *tūtiyā'* became *tutía* in Spanish. It has another form donning the Arabic **al-**, *atutía*. It is *tutia* in Portuguese and *tuzia* in Italian.

Eric: You seem to have finished discussing *tutty* that 'doth dry and clear the eyes, more than any medycynes.' Is there any other word of Arabic origin pertaining to chemistry?

Ahmad: Yes, there is. There is *alizarin* which is the red colouring matter of the madder root, i.e. 1,2-dihydroxyanthraquinone, $C_{14}H_8O_4$.

It is from *alizari* which is the levantine

---

1 *The Treasury of Health* (1585).

madder, and is from the Arabic **al-ʿuṣāraḥ**[1]
(العُصارة) meaning juice, extract, and is derived
from the verb ʿaṣara, to press, extract.

Shall I tell you another beautiful word meaning red?

Eric: Why not? Is it also of Arabic origin?

Ahmad: Of course. It is *crimson*.

Eric: I like that word very much. It is a deep red
colour, tinged with blue. I remember Shakespeare's words in *Henry V*,

> Ros'd ouer with the Virgin Crimson of
> Modestie.[2]

Ahmad: How beautiful! ... This word is from the
Arabic **qirmizī** (قِرْمِزي) which is derived from
qirmiz meaning the coccus insect from which this
is extracted. It became *cremesinus* in medieval
Latin.

The Spanish *carmesí* is very close to the
Arabic original. Italian has *cremisi* as a noun and
cremisino as an adjective. Portuguese has
carmesim. The French *cramoisi* is the farthest
from the Arabic original.

The Germanic languages have words close to

---

1 In *OED* and *CTCD*, ʿaṣārah, with an *a*, and in *NSOED*, ʿiṣārah with
an *i*. Both are wrong. *Le Petit Robert* writes it correctly with a *u*, but
writes the *s* without the dot.
2 V. ii. 323.

the Spanish-Portuguese basic form. German has *karmesin*, Dutch *karmozijn*, Swedish *karmosin*, and Danish *karmoisin*.

Another form of this word is *cramoisy*. Thomas Carlyle says, 'A blustering figure ... in ... cramoisy velvet, or other uncertain texture.'[1]

And Elizabeth Gaskell says, 'He gathered for her some velvety cramoisy roses.'[2]

Eric: Is the story of this word over?

Ahmad: No. This word is an all-rounder. It has left its traces in many domains. I have dealt with one. Please bear with me as I deal with the other domains. So lend me your ears.

Eric: Go ahead. I am all ears.

Ahmad: *Carmine* from the same Arabic word means the red colouring matter of the cochineal insect. It is also used as an adjective meaning crimson. Emma Marshall says, 'A sky where amber melted into the softest carmine.'[3]

In Spanish, it is *carmín* which is a shortened form of *carmesí*. Portuguese has *carmim* from which it derives the verb *carminar* meaning to paint carmine red. Italian has *carminio*, and French *carmin*.

---

1 *Past and Present* (1858), 105.
2 *North and South* (1855), iii.
3 *C. Kingscote*, 30.

Serbo-Croatian has *karmin,* and Russian *karmin* (кармин).

The word has given us *carminic* acid, and *carminite,* an arsenate of lead and iron, so called because of its colour.

Eric: You have not yet finished, I suppose.

Ahmad: No, not yet. The female coccus insect itself is called *kermes.* It is also applied to the oak (kermes oak) on which the insect breeds. *Kermes* or *kermesite* is a cherry-red mineral (antimony oxysulphide) so called because of its colour.

It is of course from the Arabic name of the insect **qirmiz** (قِرْمِز). It became *quermes* in Spanish and Portuguese, *chermes* in Italian, and *kermès* in French.

This word has another form with the definite article **al-,** *alkermes.* It means both the insect, and a cordial with the kermes as an ingredient. This word is now obsolete in both English and French, but is still in vogue in Spanish, Portuguese and Italian. The Spanish *alquermes* not only means the coccus insect and the cordial, but has an additional meaning of medicinal syrup. The Italian *alchermes* has only the meaning of the insect.

There is one more scion of this family. It is

armozeen. It belongs to the domain of fabrics. It is a heavy plain silk, usually black, used especially for clerical gowns and for mourning.[1] It is from the same Arabic word.

Eric: But, my dear Ahmad, what happened to the initial *c/k*-sound?

Ahmad: It has been devoured by the Egyptians. What I mean is that in Egyptian Arabic, the classical Arabic uvular *q* is reduced to a glottal stop. So *qirmizī* becomes *irmizi* which in turn became *ermisino* in Italian, and that is the source of our English word.[2]

Eric: We have digressed from our discussion of chemical terms. Shall we go back to that subject? Do you have any other chemical terms?

Ahmad: Yes, I do, but there is a lot of controversy about its etymology.

Eric: What is it?

Ahmad: It is *amalgam* which originally meant a mixture of mercury with other metal. Then it came to mean a combination of people or things. It later gave birth to the verb *amalgamate* meaning to combine or unite.

Eric: But what is its source? Is it Arabic?

Ahmad: Well, the accepted view is that the word

1 *NSOED.*
2 ibid.

is originally from the Greek *malagma* (μαλαγμα) meaning an emollient, but passed into European languages from an Arabic adaptation of the word. And the Arabic element in this word is the initial *a-* which represents the Arabic **al-**.

There is another interesting fact about this word. The Greek word *malagma* has two other forms in Arabic. These are: *malham* and *marham* both meaning ointment for wounds. The first of these forms, *malham,* passed into some of the Balkan languages through Turkish. It became *mehlem* in Bulgarian (with metathesis), and *melem* in Serbo-Croatian. Here the *h* has been lost.

Eric: Very interesting indeed.

Ahmad: I suggest that we stop for the day, and resume our discussion tomorrow *in šāʾ Allāh.*

Eric: That is a good idea. But please tell me what is *in šāʾ Allāh*?

Ahmad: It means God willing. It is interesting to note that this expression is used in Portuguese and Spanish. In the former, it is *oxalá* meaning 'may it please God!' I had occasion to tell you before that *x* in Portuguese and old Spanish is pronounced *sh*. In modern Spanish, this has been replaced by *j* which is pronounced *kh*. So

the old Spanish *oxala*[1] has now become *¡ojalá!*
Eric: O.K. We shall meet tomorrow *oxalá!* And if you want it in Spanish, then *¡ojalá!*

---

1 Dozy, *op. cit.*, p. 326.

CHAPTER 13
ALCHEMY

Ahmad: Are you ready, Eric?

Eric: Yes, I am.

Ahmad: Yesterday we were discussing chemical terms. Today, we shall discuss terms pertaining to alchemy.

Eric: Please tell me first of all, what is alchemy?

Ahmad: Alchemy is chemistry in its infancy whose chief pursuits were the transmutation of other metals into gold, and the acquisition of the elixir of life.

The word *alchemy* is from the Arabic **al-kīmiyā** (الكيميا) meaning the same, but the word *kīmiyā* itself is from the Greek *khemeia* (χημεια) whose origin is variously explained, but that is not our concern here.

In view of its pursuit of transmuting other metals into gold, the word came to mean miraculous power of transmutation. Shakespeare says in *Julius Caesar*,

That which would appear Offence in vs,

His Countenance, like richest Alchymie,
Will change to Vertue.[1]
In one of his sonnets, he says,
A glorious morning ...
Guilding pale streames with heauenly
alcumy.[2]
It also came to mean brass which was believed
to be transmuted gold, and was also applied to a
trumpet made of it. Milton says in *Paradise Lost*,
Four speedy cherubim
Put to their mouths the sounding alchymie.[3]
As a verb it meant to plate or wash with
another metal. Owen Feltham says,
It will Alchymy the gold of vertue.[4]
This verbal use is now obsolete.

The Arabic *al-kīmiyā* became *alchimia* in
medieval Latin, which is its form in Italian also.
Spanish and Portuguese have *alquimia*. French,
as usual, dropped the final -*a*, and turned the
word into *alchimie* which is the source of the
English form.

Some other European languages have the
French-English form: German and Dutch have

---

1 I. iii. 159.
2 xxxiii.
3 ii. 516.
4 *Resolves Divine*, I. xviii. (1677) 32.

alchimie, Swedish has *alkemi,* Danish *alkymi,* and Albanian *alkimi.*

Modern Greek combines its own *khemeia* (χημεια) with the Arabic article **al-** thus resulting in *alkhemeia* (αλχημεια). Russian and Serbo-Croatian have this Greek form: Russian has *alkhimia* (алхимия). Serbo-Croatian has changed the *kh* to *h*: *alhemija.*

Eric: I understand from what you said that there are other words pertaining to alchemy which are of Arabic origin.

Ahmad: Yes, you are right. An important term of alchemy is *elixir* which is an imaginary substance with which alchemists hoped to change metals into gold or make people live forever. It was sometimes identified with the 'philosopher's stone'. Chaucer says,

> The philosophre stoon
> Elixir clept, was sechen fast echoon.[1]

Milton says in *Paradise Lost,*

> What wonder then if fields and regions here
> Breathe forth elixir pure, and Rivers run
> Potable Gold.[2]

The Arabic source of this word is **al-iksīr** (الإكسير), meaning the same, which is believed to

---

1 *Chanon's Yeman's Prologue & Tale,* 310.
2 III. 607.

be a loan word in Arabic. It is probably from the Greek *xerion* (ξηριον) which means a desiccative powder for wounds.[1]

The Arabic word became *elixir* in medieval Latin. It has this same form in Spanish, Portuguese and French.[2] Italian has *elisir, elisire*.

Other European languages have the same form as in English, except that in German, it is written *Elixier*, and in Danish and Serbo-Croatian, it is written with *k* and *s* instead of *x* (*eliksir*). Modern Greek has *elixirion* (ελιξιριον), and Russian has *eleksir* (элексир).

Now I shall come to the third word of this series.

Eric: What is it?

Ahmad: It is *alembic*. It was an apparatus used in distilling. Edmund Burke says, 'The hot spirit drawn out of the alembick of hell, which in France is now so furiously boiling.'[3]

In its very early history, the word was aphetised to *limbeck*. Edmund Spenser says,

The dull drops, that from his purpled bill,
As from a limbeck, did adown distill.[4]

---

1 *Xerox* is so called because it prints using *dry* ink.
2 The French form is *élixir*.
3 *French Revolution*, 135.
4 *The Faerie Queene*, VII. vii. 31.

John Dryden says,

> I feel my Strength each Day and Hour consume
>
> Like Lillies wasting in a Lymbeck's Heat.[1]

Besides *alembic, alembicate* was also used as a verb. As distilling involves bringing out the quintessence of the original substance, and in small quantities, the verb developed metaphorical meanings like over-refining, complicating, giving sparingly, being conceited and arrogant, exaggerating, embellishing.

It is from the Arabic **al-imbīq**[2] (الإنبيق) meaning the same. The main word is an Arabicised form of the Greek *ambix* (αμβιξ) meaning a still. Due to vocalic harmony, the initial *a* changed to *i* in Arabic. It became *alambique* in Spanish and Portuguese, and *alambic* in French. Italian has the aphetised form, *lambicco*.

Many other European languages do not use this word. We have seen that Arabic got this word from Greek, but modern Greek uses its Arabic form. It has *lambikos* (λαμπικος).

Eric: Are there any more alchemical terms of Arabic origin?

Ahmad: Yes, here is another apparatus used by

---

1 *Secret Love*, I. iii.
2 In *OED* and other sources, it is *al-ambīq* (الأنبيق), which is not correct.

the alchemists. It is *aludel*. It was a pear-shaped pot used in sublimation. Ben Jonson says in *The Alchemist,*

> Let your heat, still, lessen by degrees
> To the Aludels.[1]

It is from the Arabic **al-uthāl** (الأثال) meaning the same.

Eric: Any other apparatus?

Ahmad: No. I shall now speak to you about the alchemist's name for mercury. It is *azoth*. It also means Paracelsus's universal remedy. Robert Browning says, 'Last, my good sword; ah, trusty Azoth, leapest Beneath thy master's grasp for the last time?'[2]

It is a corruption of the Spanish *azogue*, and the Portuguese *azougue* meaning mercury. They are from the Arabic **al-zāwūq**[3] (الزاووق) meaning the same. This Arabic word has two more forms: *al-zuwaq* (الزُوَق), and *al-ziʾbaq* (الزِّئبَق). The last is the original form as it is a loan word from the Persian *zhīva* (ژیوه).

From this same Spanish word comes *assogue* which was formerly applied to a Spanish vessel carrying quicksilver to America for use in the

---

1 II. iii. 624.
2 *Paracelsus*, V. Wks, 1883, I. 183.
3 *OED* writes *az-zāūq*, which is not correct.

silver-mines. It is now obsolete.

Eric: Does *azogue* have any other meaning? I am asking you this question because I heard it being used for a market-place in Spain.

Ahmad: You are perfectly right. *Azogue* is also a market-place, but it is a totally different word. It is from the Arabic **al-sūq** (السُّوق) meaning a market-place. The same Arabic word without the article gives the Spanish *zoca* meaning a square.

Eric: Let's go back to alchemy if you have some other word pertaining to this science.

Ahmad: There is one more word, but it is pseudo-Arabic.

Eric: What do you mean?

Ahmad: The bond between science and Arabic was so strong that when the German-Swiss physician and alchemist Paracelsus wanted to name the imaginary universal solvent sought by the alchemists, he came up with a meaningless word, but saw to it that it looked and sounded like Arabic. He called it *alkahest* on the pattern of *alchemy*, *alembic* and *elixir*.

Eric: That is very interesting. Can we move on now to another domain?

CHAPTER 14
ANIMAL KINGDOM

Eric: I was wondering if Arabic has given us names of animals.

Ahmad: Yes, there are some words pertaining to animals and birds which Arabic has given to European languages. One of these is *giraffe*. It is from the Arabic **zarāfah, zurāfah** (زَرَافة، زُرَافة). It became *giraffe* in Italian, *girafa* in Portuguese. In Spanish, it is *jirafa*. French, as usual, dropped the final -*a*, so the word became *girafe*, which is the source of the English word.

Other European languages have either the Portuguese or the French form, i.e. with or without the final vowel. German and Dutch have *Giraffe*, and Albanian has *gjirafë*. Danish has *giraf*, and Swedish *giraffe*.

The Serbo-Croatian *žirafa*, the Russian and Mecedonian *zhirafa* (жирафа) combine the French sound of *g* with the Portuguese form of the word. Russian has another form without the final -*a*.

Eric: What is next in your menagerie?

Ahmad: I would like to mention *civet*. As you know, it is a cat-like animal, and also the strong-smelling substance obtained from it used in making perfume. Charles Fitz-Geffrey says,

A civet-smellinge damaske rose.[1]

Shakespeare says,

Ciuet is of a baser birth then Tarre,
the verie vncleanly fluxe of a Cat.[2]

It is from the Arabic **zabād** (زَبَاد). It became *zibethum* in medieval Latin and *zapition* (ζαπιτιον) in modern Greek.

In Spanish, *civeta* is civet-cat, and *civeto* is civet perfume. In Italian, *zibetto* is the animal. In French, *civette* means both the animal and the perfume.

In German, the animal is *Zibet-katze* and in Dutch *civetkat*. In Swedish, the cat is *civett* or *sibetkatt*, and the substance is *sibet*.

In Russian, the cat is *tsivetta* (циветта), and the substance is *tsibetin* (цибетин).

Eric: I notice that you did not mention Portuguese along with Spanish as you usually do. Doesn't Portuguese have this word?

Ahmad: That is a very good question, and the

---

1 *Sir Francis Drake* (1881), 63.
2 *As You Like It*, III. ii. 69.

answer to it will reveal another important Arabic word being used in some European languages. In Portuguese, *civet* in both the senses is *algália*, and if civet-cat is meant, then *gato-de-algália* is used.

In Spanish, both *civeta/civeto* and *algalia* are used. The verb *algaliar* means to perfume with civet, and the past participle *algaliado/da* means perfumed with civet, and *algaliero* means one who likes perfumes, especially civet.

Now, the source of this word is the Arabic **al-ghāliyah** (الغالِيَة) which is a special blend of musk and ambergris with ben-oil as the base.[1] Sulaymān ibn ʿAbd al-Malik ibn Marwān is said to be the first to name this blend with this name, and he so named it as the blending was done by 'boiling'. According to another account, this credit goes to Muʿāwiyah, who named it so in view of its being very 'expensive'.[2]

Eric: Does this word have both these meanings?

Ahmad: Yes, *al-ghāliyah* may mean expensive or boiling. I should point out here that *ambergris* and *ben* are also Arabic.

Eric: O.K. Please tell me about them now before we proceed.

---

1 *Tāj al-ʿArūs*.
2 *Al-Ṣiḥāḥ* and *Tāj al-ʿArūs*.

Ahmad: First, *amber*. Formerly, *amber* meant the ash-grey strongly scented substance which is a product of the whale. Milton says,

An amber scent of odorous perfume.[1]

Now it is applied to the hard yellowish brown substance used for making ornaments and jewellery. It also means its colour as in *The traffic lights turned to amber*. Milton says,

Robed in flames and amber light.[2]

The original meaning of *amber* is now expressed by *ambergris* which is from the French *ambre gris*, i.e. grey amber. Alexander Pope says, 'Praise is like ambergris; a little whiff of it, by snatches, is very agreeable; but when a man holds a whole lump of it to his nose, it is a stink and strikes you down.'[3]

It is from the Arabic ʿambar (عَنْبَر). It became *ámbar* in Spanish, *âmbar* in Portuguese, *ambra* in Italian, and *ambre* in French which is the source of the English word. In all these languages, the word means the hard yellowish substance (the resin). To mean the original fragrant substance, the word *gris* or any other word meaning grey is added (*grigia* in Italian).

1 *Samson*, 720.
2 *L'Allegro* (61).
3 *Swift's Works* (1841), I. 837.

German and Danish use *ambra* for ambergris, and Swedish uses *grå ambra*. Dutch uses *amber* for the resin, and *grijze amber* for ambergris. Russian has *ambra* (амбра) for ambergris. By extension, it also means fragrance, perfume. Modern Greek has *ambaron* (αμπαρον) for ambergris; it uses a different word for the resin.

There are quite a few derivatives in English from *amber*. Here are some of them:

ambrette, a kind of pear with the odour of ambergris or musk.

ambrite, a yellowish grey fossil resin found in Auckland, New Zealand.

ambreate, a salt of ambreic acid.

ambrein, the chemical that forms the main constituent of ambergris.

I have finished with *amber*. Just a word regarding *ben*. It is the name of the horseradish tree. It is from **bān** (بان) in Arabic meaning the same.

Eric: I have never heard this word before. We better ban it from entering our study of Arabic words.

Ahmad: You are right... I want to round off the study of these odoriferous words with *camphor*. Its Arabic source is **kāfūr** (كافُور) meaning the same, which is ultimately from the Sanskrit *karpūram* (कर्पूरं). Though Greek took it correctly in the form of *kafura*[1] (καφουρα), it was changed to *camphora* in medieval Latin whence comes the French *camphre*, and this is the immediate source of the English form. Spanish took the word with the Arabic definite article **al-**, *alcanfor*. Portuguese has two forms, one with the **al-**, and the other without it: *alcânfora*, *cânfora*. Italian has *canfora*.

Other European languages have almost the same form. German has *Kampfer*. Dutch, Swedish and Danish have *kamfer*. Russian has *kamfara* (камфара). Even modern Greek has the common European form, *kamfora* (καμφορα).

Eric: If you have finished with this word, I propose that we go back to our menagerie.

Ahmad: Yes, let us go back. The fresh addition to our menagerie is *fennec*, a small African fox with long ears. It is from the Arabic **fanak**[2] (فَنَك). French also has *fennec*.

Spanish has *alfaneque* with the Arabic article **al-**, but it means white eagle.

Eric: That is very strange. How on earth did a four-legged animal turn into a winged creature?

---

1 H. G. Liddell & R. Scott, *A Greek-English Lexicon.*
2 *OED* and *CTCD* write this word with e's (*fenek*), which is not correct as Arabic does not have this vowel.

Ahmad: It is very simple. A kind of hawk in north Africa which hunts the fennec is called bāz al-fanak (بازُ الفَنَك), 'fennec hawk'. Spanish shortened this word by omitting the first element.[1]

As we have taken wing, I shall speak to you now about a bird. Of course you know the albatross.

Eric: Yes, of course. Coleridge made it famous through his *Ancient Mariner*.

Ahmad: That's right. Let's first of all take *alcatras*.

Eric: But what's *alcatras*? I have never heard of it in my life.

Ahmad: Yes, you may not have heard of it. The word is now obsolete. In Spanish and Portuguese, *alcatraz* means a pelican. In English also, it was applied to the pelican or frigate-bird.

The generally held view is that *alcatras* is a corruption of the Portuguese *alcatruz* which means the bucket of a water-wheel. The pelican was so called, according to these sources, in view of the fact that it draws up water in its great beak in order to carry it to its young in the desert. And this *alcatruz* is a corruption of the Arabic al-qādūs (القَادُوس) meaning the bucket of a water-wheel.

---

1 Dozy, *op. cit.*, p. 105.

But according to *NSOED*, *alcatras* is the Arabic **al-ghaṭṭās** (الغَطَّاس) meaning the diver. Either way, *alcatras* is of Arabic origin.

Eric: When do we go from *alcatras* to Coleridge's *albatross*?

Ahmad: Soon. In fact, *albatross* is the same as *alcatras*. We have seen how *amiral* was changed to *admiral* because of its supposed Latin pedigree. The same thing happened to *alcatras*. Supposing that *alcatras* was derived from the Latin *albus* meaning white, they changed *alcatras* to *albatross*.

Eric: Don't you have the name of any auspicious bird?

Ahmad: Well, I have a bird in mind. It is ... not auspicious, and it is not inauspicious either. It is neutral with regard to this aspect.

Eric: No problem. But what bird is it?

Ahmad: It is *papejay* or *popinjay* meaning a parrot. There are quite a lot of spellings of the word. Now, this word is either obsolete or archaic. Figuratively, it also means a vain affected person. Sir Walter Scott says, 'The fond fool was decked in a painted coat, and jangling as pert and as proud as any popinjay.'[1]

---

1 *Ivanhoe*, III. v. 126.

Eric: I remember that Shakespeare also uses this word in *Henry IV Part One*, but he says *popingay* instead of *popinjay*.

Ahmad: You are right. *Popingay* is the original form. It is from the Arabic **babbaghā'** (بَبَّغَاء) or **babghā'** (بَبْغَاء) meaning parrot. In all the European languages, the *b* became *p*. It became *papagayo* or *papagaya* in Spanish, *papagaio* in Portuguese, and *papagallo* in Italian. French as usual dropped the final *o*, and changed the word to *papegai*. Old French had two forms: *papegay* and *papingay*. English took the second form, but made two cosmetic changes: it changed the first *a* to *o*, and the *g* to *j* thus turning *papingay* into *popinjay*. The second change was made to connect the word with *jay*, the noisy bird with bright feathers.

Eric: We have thereby domesticated the word.

Ahmad: Exactly, as you did with *admiral*. Let's now see its form in other European languages. Most have the French form, some have adopted the Spanish form, and some others, the Italian form.

The German *Papagei*, Dutch *papagaai*, and Serbo-Croatian *papagai* are based on the French form. The Danish *papegøje* and Swedish *papegoja* are close to the Spanish form.

It is *papagal* in Rumanian, *papagall* in Albanian, *papagal* (папагал) in Macedonian, and *papagalos* (παπαγαλος) in modern Greek. And all these words represent the Italian form.

Russian has a slightly abnormal form. It is *popugay* (попугай) which resembles the French form except for the *o* and *u* in the first and second syllables. Polish has *papuga*.

Eric: A beautiful bird with an interesting name... Any other bird with an Arabic name?

Ahmad: Yes, there is. It is *marabou* or *marabout* which is a large West African stork. The word is also applied to the soft white downy feathers found under the wings and tail of this bird, used for trimming hats and dresses. The *Illustrated London News* said, 'Ladies who rejoice in the soft fluffy white trimming called marabout.'[1] In view of its whiteness, it is also applied to an exceptionally white kind of raw silk.

Eric: You have not yet mentioned its Arabic origin.

Ahmad: I wanted to do it at the end, for it is connected with another word. *Marabout* originally meant a Muslim hermit in North Africa. It is from the Arabic **murābiṭ** (مُرَابِط) which originally meant a garrisoned soldier. Then it came

---

1 Oct. 11, 1884, 338/3

to mean a soldier-hermit, and then just a hermit.

This word became *morabito* in Spanish which is very close to the Arabic original. But in Portuguese, it underwent a change and became *marabuto*, and by dropping the final -*o*, French turned it into *marabout*. In French, it not only means a Muslim hermit, but also a witch-doctor. And the verb *marabouter* means to bewitch.

By extension, it is also applied to the tomb of a saint as in *la tour carrée d'un minaret, le dôme d'un marabout* (Perec).[1]

Eric: But why was the stork called *marabout*?

Ahmad: It is said that the posture of the bird resembles that of a hermit while praying!

Eric: Let's take leave of hermits and witch-doctors. Surely there can't be any other animal or bird with an Arabic name.

Ahmad: Yes, there is, but it is only half Arabic.

Eric: How can a word be half Arabic? Please tell me the word immediately.

Ahmad: It is *alpaca*, a Peruvian animal akin to the llama. According to WNUUD, the Peruvian name of the animal is *paco* to which the Arabic definite article **al-** has been prefixed.

Eric: But how can a Peruvian word have the Arabic definite article prefixed to it?

---

1 *Le Petit Robert.*

Ahmad: It is simple. There are a sizeable number of Arabs living in Latin America. They must have used the word first, and it caught on.
Eric: Plausible. Ahmad, isn't it now time we end our visit to the zoo?
Ahmad: Please bear with me for a few more minutes.
Eric: Do you have another animal?
Ahmad: Yes, one more, and it is a very important one.
Eric: What animal is it?
Ahmad: It is *alfin*, the elephant.
Eric: But we don't use this word, do we?
Ahmad: We don't use it anymore, but we used to. It is the former name of the bishop in chess. In his book *The Game and Playe of the Chesse*, William Caxton says, 'The alphyn goeth alwey corner-wyse.'[1] Though we no longer use it in English, it is still used in other languages. In Spanish, it is *alfil*. In old French, it was *aufin* with the change of *l* to *u* as we have seen before. But in the sixteenth century, this word changed to *fou*.

It is from the Arabic **al-fīl** (الفيل), the elephant. Note that the original *l* has been changed to *n* in

---

1 IV. iv. K8.

the French and English forms of the word.

Eric: So the use of this word is confined only to chess as I can see.

Ahmad: No, it is found outside the chessboard also. In Spanish, ivory is *marfil* which is a corruption of the Arabic nāb al-fīl (نَابُ الفِيل) literally meaning elephant tusk. Portuguese has further corrupted it to *marfim*. Rumanian uses *fildeş* which is from the Turkish *fildiş*, and is made up of the Arabic *fīl* and the Turkish *diş* meaning tooth. Albanian also uses this word. It is written *fildish*. Even modern Greek has this Turkish word. As Greek has no *sh* sound, it has changed the word to *fildisi* (φιλντισι).

I have yet to tell you about the Italian word for bishop in chess.

Eric: Does it also come from the elephant?

Ahmad: No, it comes from the horse.

Eric: But Ahmad, you said you had only one more animal.

Ahmad: Yes, but as the word for bishop comes from both of them, they may be regarded as one.

Eric: You have tricked me into listening to this. O.K. Go ahead.

Ahmad: The Italian *alfiere* is from the Arabic al-fāris (الفارس) meaning a horseman or a knight, and is derived from *faras* (فرس), a horse. It

passed into old French in the form of *alfier*
meaning a standard-bearer.

Eric: And what happened to its final *s?*

Ahmad: That is a very good question. The
French dropped it thinking it to be the *s* of
plural. And this Arabic word minus the *s* was
imported by the Italians, and it means a
standard-bearer, and also the bishop in chess.

Even English had this word in the form of
alferes meaning a standard-bearer. Its *s* was also
often treated as that of plural as can be seen
from this 1679 text, 'There are no lieutenants in
all the Flanders companies, only Captains and
Alfara's.'[1]

Eric: Shall we now leave the animal kingdom,
Ahmad? Can we now move back to human
habitation?

Ahmad: Of course we can, but before we do that,
we must discuss a delicacy of certain animals.

Eric: What is it?

Ahmad: It is *alfalfa.*

Eric: *Alfalfa!* What does it mean?

Ahmad: *Oxford Advanced Learner's Dictionary*
defines it as 'a plant used for feeding farm
animals. The young plants are sometimes also

---

1 Thomas B. and Thomas J. Howell, *Cobbett's Complete Collection of
State Trials* (1816), VII. 347.

eaten by people as a vegetable.'

Eric: So it is a common delicacy.

Ahmad: It would seem so. Now for its origin. It is from the Arabic **al-fiṣfiṣah** (الفِصْفِصَة) meaning the same.

Eric: It has shrunk considerably on arrival in Europe.

Ahmad: Maybe due to the cold weather. But the shrinkage is more in the Portuguese *alfafa*. Spanish has *alfalfa* whence comes the English form. It had an older form which was *alfalfez*[1] where the Arabic ṣ is represented by the z. We also have half of this word.

Eric: What do you mean?

Ahmad: I mean the word *alfa*. Is it not half of *alfalfa*?

Eric: It sure is. But what does it mean?

Ahmad: It is a kind of grass also known as esparto grass. It is grown in Spain and N. Africa, and is used for making paper, baskets, cordage, etc. It is from the Arabic **ḥalfā'** (حَلْفاء) meaning the same, and that is why it is also called *halfa* with an *h*. French has *alfa* and *alpha*. In German, it is *Alfagras, Halfagras*.

---

1 Dozy, *op. cit.*, pp. 100-101.

CHAPTER 15
MISCELLANEOUS

Eric: At last you have finished with the manger and the menagerie.

Ahmad: Yes. Eric, you spoke of shrinkage, and I have a very interesting example of this. It is the word *ream*.

Eric: Don't tell me it is Arabic.

Ahmad: I need not tell you that. Its history will tell.

Eric: O.K. Please tell me its history.

Ahmad: Its source is the Arabic **rizmah** (رِزْمَة) meaning a bundle. The Italian *risma* is very close to the Arabic original. Spanish and Portuguese have *resma*. French, the great trimmer of words, swallowed the *z* of the Arabic original, and changed the *i* to *a*. And the result is *rame*. English slightly modified this, and turned it into *ream*. The Dutch *riem* is also from this form.

If French has swallowed the *z*, some Germanic languages have swallowed the *m*. German has *Ries* for the original *riesma*. Note that the entire syllable has been omitted. Danish and Swedish have *ris*.

Eric: This is a very strange word. Four words, *risma, rame, ream* and *ris* have all been born of a single word.

Ahmad: You are right. But here is another word which has undergone more shrinkage than the former.

Eric: Which word is that?

Ahmad: *Azure*.

Eric: Oh, what a beautiful word! Pope says,

Celestial azure brightning in her eyes.[1]

Ahmad: And Byron says,

The vast and sullen swell

Of ocean's alpine azure.[2]

Eric: Shakespeare says,

Her azure veins, her alabaster skin.[3]

Ahmad: Shelley says,

It was the azure time of June.[4]

Eric: Both of us are waxing lyrical. Let's come down to the prosaic world of etymology. Now, please tell me its Arabic source so that we may find out the percentage of shrinkage it has

---

1 *Odyssey*, I. 408.
2 *The Island*, III. iii.
3 *Lucrece*, 419.
4 *Rosalind and Helen*, 957.

undergone.

Ahmad: The Arabic source of this word is **al-lāzaward** (اللازَوَرد) meaning the same. It is from the Persian *lājward* or *lāžward* (لاجْورد، لاژورد). It is the precious stone of blue colour known also as *lapis lazuli*.

During its transition to European languages, it lost the article **al-** and the first letter *l*, and the last letter *d*. In Italian, it became *azzurro*, and in French, *azur* whence comes the English *azure*.

Spanish and Portuguese changed the *r* to *l*, and the word in these two languages is *azul*.

Some east European languages have retained the initial *l* of the word. Polish has *lazur*. Russian also has this form, *lazur'* (лазурь). In English also, *lazure* was used by writers in the 17th century, but is now obsolete.

Latin not only retained the initial *l*, but also changed the *r* to *l*. So the word became *lazulum* which we find in the name of the precious stone *lapis lazuli*.

Have you noticed, Eric, the extent of shrinkage in this poor word?

Eric: Yes, it is tremendous. It seems to have done slim-fast exercises. But what it lost in size, it has gained in beauty.

Ahmad: As we are studying precious stones, I

should tell you of another stone which is a
delicate rose-red variety of the spinel ruby.

Eric: What is it called?

Ahmad: It is called *balas*. It is from the Arabic
balakhš (بَلْخْش) meaning the same, which is from
badakhš in Persian, a shortened form of *Badakh-
šān* in Afghanistan where it is found.

In medieval Latin, *balakhš* became *balascus*
with metathesis. This is the source of *balascio* in
Italian, *balaxe* in Portuguese, and *balais* in
French whence comes the English *balas*.

Eric: We have studied the etymologies of two
precious stones. Would you like to tell me about
any other precious or unprecious stones?

Ahmad: Yes. I would like to tell you about
another stone. It is not precious in the accepted
sense, but it may be more precious in a different
sense.

Eric: More precious than precious stones? What
can that be?

Ahmad: It is *bezoar*. It is a stony concretion
found in the stomachs of goats, antelopes,
llamas, chamois, etc., formerly esteemed as an
antidote to all poisons. By extension, it came to
mean any antidote. Edward Topsell says, 'The
juice of Apples being drunk, and Endive, are the
proper bezoar against the venom of a Phalan-

gie."[1]

It is from the Arabic **bāzahr**[2] (بازَهْر) meaning a stone with antidotal qualities. It is originally from the Persian *pādzahr* (پادْزهْر) meaning an antidote. In Spanish, it became *bazaar, bezar,* and *bezoar.* Portuguese has *bezoar.* French has a *d* at the end of the word, *bézoard.* This *d* appears in the English adjectival form, *bezoardic.*

Eric: Is *almanac* an Arabic word? It starts with **al-**, and looks like an Arabic word.

Ahmad: Yes, it is. An almanac is a calendar with astronomical data and calculations. Its Arabic source is **al-manākh** (المَنَاخ) which is a less frequently used form of *al-munākh.*[3] Originally meaning a place where camels live, it later acquired the sense of a place with a special climatic condition. By extension, it also means climatic conditions of a particular place. It is this sense of the word which developed in European languages to mean a calendar containing astronomical data.

It is *almanaque* in Spanish and Portuguese, *almanacco* in Italian and *almanach* in French

---

1 *The Historie of Serpents* (1608), 775.
2 Ibn al-Bayṭār, *op. cit.,* 1:81, *Muḥīṭ al-Muḥīṭ,* p. 25.
3 *Tāj al-ʿArūs,* نوخ.

where the final *ch* is not pronounced.

Other European languages mostly have the French-English form. German has *Almanach*, Dutch *almanac*, Swedish *almanack*, and Danish *almanak*.

Russian and Macedonian have the guttural *kh* instead of the velar *k*. It is *al'manakh* (альманах) in Russian, and *almanakh* (алманах) in Macedonian. Serbo-Croatian has changed the final *kh* to *h: almanah*. Albanian has the English form *almanak*.

I have finished with *almanac*, Eric. But I am reminded of a couple of related words that may interest you.

Eric: What are they?

Ahmad: One of them is **taqwīm** (تقويم) which is the Arabic word for calendar. In Italian, this has become *taccuino*, and means agenda, almanac, memorandum-book, notebook. It is not used in other languages.

Eric: And the other?

Ahmad: The second word is *monsoon* which is the seasonal wind prevailing in the Indian Ocean. The Dutch and the Portuguese were the first to record this word. The 16th century Portuguese form of the word was *moução*. Now it is *monção*. The present-day Dutch form is *moes-*

son, but formerly it was *monssoen*. In French, it is *mousson*. Italian has *monsone* and Spanish, *monzón*.

It is from the Arabic **mawsim** (مَوْسِم) meaning season.

Most of the other languages have the form with two *n*'s. Serbo-Croatian, German, Swedish, and Danish have *monsun*.

Macedonian has *monsun* (монсун). But Russian has the French form, *musson* (муссон), but it is pronounced without the nasalization.

Eric: I have been thinking about *almanac*. It is interesting to note how a word denoting a place where camels live has come to mean tables comprising astronomical data.

Ahmad: That is semantic change. 'Translation' during Shakespeare's time meant 'transformation'. Don't you remember that when Bottom emerged from the 'green room' with an asinine head, his colleagues exclaimed, 'Bottom! ... thou art translated!'[1]

Eric: Yes, I do.

Ahmad: The word *translation* reminds me of a very interesting word.

Eric: What is it?

Ahmad: It is *dragoman* meaning an interpreter.

---

1 *Midsummer Night's Dream*, III. i.

It has many forms including *dracoman* and *druggerman*. Alexander Pope says,

Pity, you was not Druggerman at Babel![1]

It is from the Arabic **tarjumān** (تَرْجُمَان) meaning an interpreter. It has two more forms, *turjumān*, and *tarjamān*. It became *dragumannus* in medieval Latin. It is *dragomán* in Spanish, *dragomano* in Portuguese, *dragomanno* in Italian, and *drogman* in French. This form of the word with a *g* is from a Yemeni dialect which pronounces the Arabic letter ج (*j*) as a voiced velar stop (*g*). It is interesting to note that the same word has been adopted in these languages with the classical Arabic pronunciation of *j*.

Eric: But do they have *t* or *d* at the beginning of the word?

Ahmad: The various forms of this word based on the classical pronunciation have *t*. Here are these forms:

In Spanish, it is *trujamán* or *triujimán*. As a trader speaking more than one language can sell his goods more effectively, the word has come to mean an expert trader. It also retains its original meaning of an interpreter. The verb *trujamanear* also reflects these meanings. It means to act as an interpreter; to act as a broker; to exchange,

---

1 *Satires of Dr Donne Versified*, IV. 83.

barter, trade. And the noun *trujamanía* means brokering or brokerage.

Eric: This is a very interesting semantic development indeed.

Ahmad: Yes. We will now see this word in other languages as well.

In Portuguese, it is *trugimão*, or *turgimão*, and means an interpreter (especially in the Near East and Iran).

In Italian, it is *turcimanno*, and means an interpreter.

In French, it is *truchement*. It means an interpreter and also a go-between.

In English, it became *truchman*, and has several alternate spellings. Samuel Butler says, 'He is a Truch-Man, that interprets between learned Writers and gentle Readers.'[1]

A very interesting feature of this word is that a female interpreter is called a *truchwoman*. And a *truch spirite* is a spirit acting as interpreter or messenger.[2] Both these words are now obsolete.

Another interesting fact about this word is that it has been corrupted to *trenchman* which apparently is a misreading of *treuchman*. An 1879 text reads, 'A strong active young fellow ...

---

1 *Remains*, II, 405.
2 *OED*.

acted as our trenchman.'[1]

Eric: *Truchwoman!* You could just as well say *Mussulwoman* for a female Mussulman.

Ahmad: It has already been said. Would you believe that?

Eric: By whom?

Ahmad: By more than one person. Byron for example says, 'The poor dear Mussulwomen whom I mention.'[2]

Eric: Is *Mussulman* an Arabic word?

Ahmad: No, it isn't. It is a Persian word based on the Arabic *Muslim.*

Eric: Ahmad, are there words concerning Islam which are in day-to-day use and have no reference to religion?

Ahmad: Yes, there are. We have the word *mecca* which is the name of the Muslim holy city of Mecca where millions go for pilgrimage each year. It has come to mean any place regarded by a group of people as a centre of attraction. We speak of *mecca of our hopes, mecca of his dreams, mecca for bird-watchers.* Some other languages also use this expression. The French say, *Ces îles sont la Mecque des surfers* (These islands are the mecca for surfers), and the

---

1 Boddam-Whetham, *Roraima and British Guiana,* 147.
2 *Beppo,* lxxvii.

Germans say, *das Mekka für Golfers* (the mecca for golfers).

There is another important word, but now it is obsolete.

Eric: What is it?

Ahmad: It is *maumet*. It has more than twenty-five forms including *mammet*.

Eric: I know this word. Shakespeare uses it to mean dolls in *Henry IV Part One*. He says,

This is no world

To play with Mammets.[1]

Ahmad: Exactly. But the word originally means a false god, or an idol. Sir Thomas More speaks of 'the ydolles and mammettes of the paganes.'[2] By extension, it was also applied to a person or a thing that usurps the place of God in human affections. Chaucer says,

◦   Euery floryn in his cofre is his mawmet.[3]

Eric: It was also used as a term of contempt. Shakespeare in *Romeo And Juliet* says,

A wretched whyning foole,

A puling mammet.[4]

Ahmad: You are right. In this sense it is still in

---

1 II. iv. 89.

2 *Dialogue Heresyes*, I, Works 119/2.

3 *The Parson's Tale*, 749.

4 III. v. 184.

vogue in certain dialects. From *mammet* was derived *mammetry* meaning idolatry. William Lambarde says, 'Let the souldiours of Satan and superstitious Mawmetrie, howl, and cry out...'[1]

Eric: Ahmad, this word comes from the name *Muḥammad*, doesn't it?

Ahmad: Yes, sadly it does come from his name. In fact the earliest form of the word used in 1205 was *mahimet*. The word acquired this meaning due to the common medieval notion that Prophet Muhammad was worshipped as god by the Muslims which, of course, is false.

Eric: Thank God the word is now obsolete.

Ahmad: Yes. There is another form of this word, but in a different context. The mysterious idol the Knights Templars were accused of worshipping was called *Baphomet*. Carlyle says, 'My Spiritual New-birth, or Baphometic Fire-baptism.'[2] This is another corruption of the name of *Muḥammad*.

Eric: Whether it was the result of mischief or ignorance, it was very unfortunate.

Ahmad: The Knights Templars remind me of *talisman*.

Eric: Is that also an Arabic word?

---

1 *A Perambulation of Kent* (1826) 268.
2 *Sartor Resartus*, II. vii.

Ahmad: Yes. It is from the Arabic ṭilasm (طِلَسْم) or ṭillasm[1], meaning the same, which is a loan word from Greek. In classical Greek, *telesma* (τελεσμα) meant payment, tax, certificate. But later it came to mean a consecrated object endowed with magical virtue to avert evil. The final -*an* in *talisman* remains unexplained.

The word is found in other European languages also. It is *talismán* in Spanish, *talismã* in Portuguese and *talismano* in Italian. French has the same form as the English. Most of the other languages have the French-English form.

Eric: O.K. What's next?

Ahmad: How about a short excursion to the museum?

Eric: What for? To see mummies?

Ahmad: You said, 'to see mummies'.

Eric: Don't tell me you have spotted an Arabic word there.

Ahmad: Yes, I have for sure. *Mummy* is Arabic. It is from the Arabic **mūmiyā** (مُومِيا) meaning the same. It is a loan word from Persian, and is derived from *mūm* meaning wax (which was

---

1 *OED* and other sources write this word *ṭilsam*, which does not exist in Arabic. The vulgar pronunciation of the word is *ṭalsam*. The two pronunciations given above are the ones mentioned by al-Zabīdī in *Tāj al-ʿArūs*.

used in embalming). This Arabic word became *múmia* in Portuguese, *mummia* in Italian, *momia* in Spanish, and *momie* in French. Germanic languages have the French-English form. German, Danish and Swedish have *mumie*, and Dutch has *mummie*.

Slavic languages have the Romance form. Russian has *mumiya* (мумня), Serbo-Croatian has *mumija*, and Polish has *mumia*. Modern Greek also has this form, *mumia* (μουμια).

CHAPTER 16
UTENSILS

Eric: You have mentioned before that the Italian *bricco* meaning coffee pot is of Arabic origin. Are there other words denoting utensils?

Ahmad: Yes, there are some. One of the commonest words is *jar*. Formerly, it was also used as a measure of capacity varying according to the commodity.

It is from the Arabic **jarrah** (جَرَّة) which is an earthen vessel. It became *jarra* in Portuguese, *giara* in Italian, and *jarro* in Spanish which also has *jarrón* for a large jar.

The Spanish *aliara* meaning a horn goblet and *zalona* meaning a large earthen jar also come from the same Arabic word.[1]

Eric: I think the *jar* in *ajar* as *to leave the door ajar* has nothing to do with our *jar*.

Ahmad: No, it is a different word. It is the English word *char* meaning a turn. It is from the old English *cyrr*, *cerr* with the same meaning.

---

1 Dozy, *op. cit.*, 129, 362.

Eric: Any other word denoting a vessel?

Ahmad: Yes, *carafe* which, as you know, is a glass container in which water or wine is served at meals. *OED* says, 'The word has long been in common use in Scotland: in England it is of later appearance, and often treated as still French. Also vulgarly corrupted to *craft, croft.*'

The word is from the Arabic **gharrāfah** (غَرَّافة) derived from *gharafa*, to draw water with the hand or with a vessel. It became *garrafa* in Spanish and Portuguese, *caraffa* in Italian, and *carafe* in French. The English *carafe* is from the French form.

Spanish has two more forms: *garrafilla* for a small carafe, and *garrafón* for a large one. But in French, *carafon* has acquired the meaning of a small carafe.

In Portuguese, *garrafa* means a bottle, and in the sense of a carafe, it is called *garrafa para água*. The word has quite a few derivatives in Portuguese.

Eric: Do they refer to the carafe or to the bottle?

Ahmad: They refer to the bottle. Here are some of these derivatives:

garrafada, a bottleful.

garrafal, bottle-shaped.

garrafão, a large bottle, a demijohn.

garrafaria, bottle rack, wine-cellar.

garrafeiro, bottle-maker, bottle dealer.

garafinha, vial.

Eric: Is the word used in other European languages?

Ahmad: Yes, in most of them. German has *Karaffe* which is close to the Italian form. So also is the modern Greek *karafa* (καραφα). The Dutch and Swedish have the French-English form (*karaff, karaf*). The Danish *karaffel* reflects the Spanish diminutive *garrafilla*. The Russian *grafin* (графин) is also based on the Spanish diminutive with the change of *l* to *n*, and the dropping of the final *a*. The Albanian *garafë* reflects the original Spanish form.

Eric: Is there any other word belonging to this domain?

Ahmad: Yes, there is another word. It is *tass* and means a cup or a small goblet. It is *tassie* in the Scottish dialect. Burns says,

> Ye'll bring me here a pint of wine,
> A server and a silver tassie.[1]

It is from the Arabic **ṭās** (طاس) which is a copper drinking-cup.[2] It became *taza* in Spanish, and

---

1 *Homely Ballad* (in *Burns' Poems* [1834] II. 229, *note*).

2 *OED* and other sources mention that it is from the Arabic طس which is from the Persian تشت. But there is no evidence for this theory. The word طاس is an independent word as mentioned by all the authorities of Arabic.

means a cup, basin of a fountain, large wooden bowl, cup guard of a sword.

It is *tazza* in Italian, and means a cup, mug, basin. *Tazza di fontana* means basin of a fountain.

In Portuguese, it is *taça*, and means cup, goblet. By extension it also means a trophy.

French as usual dropped the final *a*, and turned it to *tasse* which is the source of the English word.

Eric: Is the word found in other languages as well?

Ahmad: Yes, in some of them. German has *Tasse* meaning a cup, e.g. *eine Tasse Tee*, a cup of tea.

Russian has *taz* (таз) meaning basin. It also means pelvis which seems to be an extension of the first meaning.

Modern Greek *tasi*, *tasaki* (τασι, τασακι) means saucer, and by extension, ash tray.

CHAPTER 17
MORE MISCELLANEOUS

Eric: We have seen examples of Arabic words used in some European languages but not in English. A little while ago you mentioned *taccuino* which is found only in Italian. Can we discuss some examples of this kind?

Ahmad: Sure. There are two types of words:

a) words which are used in English and some other European languages, but their use in English is very limited;

b) words which are not at all used in English, but are used in other European languages.

First, we shall take an example of the first category.

Divan in English means, *inter alia*, a council of state, a council-chamber with cushioned seats, an Eastern couch, etc. But it has not been integrated into English. It has a foreign look, and a foreign connotation. One of the meanings of the Arabic **dīwān** (ديوان) is customs.[1] This is the meaning which caught on in other European languages. In French, it is *douane* meaning customs, custom-house, etc., and *douanier* (*fem.*, *douanière*) is a customs officer.

In Italian, it is *dogana* meaning customs and custom-house, and *doganiere* is a customs officer. The verb *doganare* means to impose customs duties.

Spanish and Portuguese have this word with the Arabic definite article **al-** prefixed. In Spanish, it is *aduana* meaning custom-house, and *aduanero* means a customs officer. The verb *aduanar* means to enter goods at the custom-house, to pay customs duty.

Portuguese also has the same form, *aduana*, meaning custom-house, customs, custom-duties, and the verb *aduanar* means to clear at a custom-house.

Albanian and Esperanto also use the Italian form of the word. It is *doganë* in Albanian, and *dogano* in Esperanto.

Eric: I know the French word *douane*, but I never thought it could be Arabic.

Ahmad: Here is another example. The Arabic

---

1 *Riḥlah ibn Jubayr*, pp. 44-45.

word **miskīn** (مِسْكِين) meaning poor, miserable, humble is very much a living word in the Romance languages. But in English it is rarely used. It means mean, sordid, shabby. Charles Kingsley says, 'The mesquin and scrofulous visages, which crowd our alleys.'[1]

The Arabic word became *mezquino* in Spanish. It has retained many of its original meanings like poor, indigent, penurious, and has developed many more which are a corollary to the original meanings like diminutive, avaricious, covetous, niggardly, paltry, mean, lean, petty, etc.

The noun *mezquinidad* means poverty, penury, indigence; avarice; meanness. And the adverb *mezquinamente* means miserably.

It became *mesquinho* in Portuguese, which also has retained the original meanings like poor, indigent, wretched, pitiful, and has developed a wealth of other meanings like niggard, skinflint; mean, shabby; insignificant; intractable; coy; mistrustful.

The noun *mesquinharia* (also *mesquinhez*) has some of these meanings like indigence, wretchedness; insignificance; shabbiness, meanness.

---

1 *At last: a Christmas in the West Indies*, ii.

The verb *mesquinhar* deals only with second-ary meanings like to be stingy; to evade an issue, be evasive.

From the meaning of being intractable is derived *mesquinhador* meaning a horse that refuses to be bridled.

The Italian *meschino* means a wretched crea-ture, a miserable fellow. But it also has meanings like mean, paltry, shabby. The expression *fare una figura meschina* means to cut a poor figure.

The noun *meschineria* (also *meschinità*) means misery; stinginess; meanness, shabbiness.

The diminutive *meschinello* means poor, wretched, shabby. And the adverb *meschina-mente* means meanly, poorly, shabbily.

By the time the word arrived in France, it had lost all vestiges of the original meanings. Now the French *mesquin* just means shabby, paltry, mean. And the noun *mesquinerie* means meanness, shabbiness. And this is the meaning that the English form of the word has also inherited from its French source.

Eric: Shall we move on to the second category?

Ahmad: Yes. Here is an interesting example. One of the words which Portuguese and Spanish have taken from Arabic is the preposition ḥattā (حتى) meaning *until.* It became *até* in Portuguese as in *até agora*, till now, *até o dia de hoje*, till this day.

Spanish changed it to *hasta* by inserting an *s* before the *t* as in *hasta ahora* meaning hitherto, until now, and *hasta la vista*, good-bye, until we meet again.

Eric: That is really interesting. Is there any other grammatical element that European languages have borrowed from Arabic?

Ahmad: Let me see. ... Yes, there is. The adjectival form of a noun (called *nasab* in Arabic) is formed in Arabic by suffixing -*iyy* *(un)* which is reduced to *ī* in the spoken language. English and some other languages use this Arabic suffix in the adjectival form of the names of certain countries like *Iraqi*, *Israeli*, *Pakistani*, *Kuwaiti*, etc.

Eric: That is right. I never thought it was of Arabic origin.

Ahmad: I would like to mention a few more words of Arabic origin that are used in some European languages but not in English.

Eric: Please go ahead.

Ahmad: Certain Arabic words passed into some of the Balkan languages through Turkish.

- The Arabic word for a grocer is **baqqāl** (بَقَّال). It originally meant a greengrocer,

and is derived from *baql* meaning pot-
herb. This has become *bakales* (μπακαλης)
in modern Greek, *băcan* (with an *n*) in
Rumanian, *bakalin* in Serbo-Croatian,
bakal (бакал) in Macedonian, *bakall* in
Albanian, and *bakaleyshchik* (бакалейщик)
in Russian, all meaning grocer.

- Another Arabic word which is found in
many Balkan languages is **mušamma͑**
(مُشَمَّع) meaning oilcloth, and is derived
from *šam͑* (شَمع) meaning wax. It is
muşama in Rumanian, *mušema* in Serbo-
Croatian, *mushama* in Albanian, and
musamas (μουσαμας) in modern Greek.

- A very strange word in Rumanian is
muşteriu for a customer which is from the
Arabic **muštari(n)** (مُشتر) meaning a buyer.
It is *müşteri* in Turkish which is the source
of the Rumanian word.

Eric: Can you give a couple of words from
Spanish or Portuguese, or both?

Ahmad: Yes, of course, but both these languages
are so full of Arabic words that I need some time
to pick and choose from them. ... Let me think
for a while. ... Yes, I have thought of a word. It is
the Spanish *alfombra* meaning a carpet. Metaphorically, it also means a cover and ornament.

It is also applied to measles, likening the body covered with red spots to a carpet. In Portuguese, in addition to carpet, it also means a lawn.

Eric: And what is its Arabic source?

Ahmad: Its Arabic source is **al-khumrah** (الْخُمْرَة) which is a small prayer carpet made of palm leaves. The word occurs in some *aḥādīth*.[1]

Eric: But the *kh* sound has become *f* in Spanish and Portuguese. Is this a normal phonetic change?

Ahmad: That is a very good question. Yes, in many Spanish and Portuguese words of Arabic origin, both *kh* and *ḥ* of Arabic have become *f*. We have already seen that the Arabic *al-kharrūb* became *alfarroba* in Portuguese. Here is another word with *kh*, **al-khilāl** (الْخِلَال), a pin or a toothpick. This became *alfiler* in Spanish meaning a pin. Note that the second *l* has changed to *r*. This is because of dissimilation. In Portuguese, the word has been licked out of shape. It has become *alfinete* with the first *l* changing to *n*, and the second to *t*!

Eric: This is a strange sound change. Don't you think so?

---

1 *Aḥādīth* is the plural of *ḥadīth* which is a record of actions and sayings of Prophet Muḥammad (may peace and blessings of Allah be on him).

Ahmad: Yes, it is, but it will look less strange if you know that Spanish also changes *f* to *h* in certain words as can be seen from the following examples:

- The Latin *farina* (flour) is *harina* in Spanish, but the Portuguese *farinha* retains the *f*.
- The Latin *furnax* (oven), which has become *furnace* in English, is *horno* in Spanish, but *forno* in Portuguese.

Examples abound.

Eric: Has this change taken place in any Arabic word?

Ahmad: Yes, but in only a few words. A very good example is the Arabic word **al-funduq** (الفُنـدُق) meaning a hotel. This has become *alhóndiga* in Spanish, but the meaning has changed. It means a public granary. Portuguese, on the other hand, has retained the *f*. The Portuguese *alfândega* means a custom-house. Another word for a custom-house is *aduana* which we have already seen.

Eric: Let's go back to *alfombra* which you said is from *al-khumraĥ*. Where did this *b* come from in *alfombra*?

Ahmad: This *b* was not in the deal; it is a bonus. As you know, *b* and *m* are from the same point of articulation, i.e. from the lips. The difference between them is that *b* is orally articulated while *m* is nasally articulated. So in certain words, a *b* is formed after the articulation of *m*, as if the remaining breath after the articulation of *m* comes out from the mouth producing *b*. A very good example of this in English is the word *number* which is ultimately from the Latin *numerus*. The German *Nummer* has no *b*. I will give you two more examples. Our *limb* is from the old English *lim*, and *thumb* from the old English *thúma*. But the *b* in these two words is now only for show.

Eric: What an excellent exposition!

Ahmad: Thank you. There is another word for a carpet in Spanish and Portuguese. It is *alcatifa*.

Eric: From the initial *al-*, it is obvious that the word is Arabic.

Ahmad: Exactly. It is from the Arabic **al-qaṭīfah** (القطيفة) which is a tissue with a velvety texture.

Eric: Can you give me an example of a Spanish word where the Arabic *kh* has not changed to *f*?

Ahmad: Yes, there are a number of words where the Arabic *kh* has not changed to *f*. A good example is *almohada* meaning a pillow which is from the Arabic **al-mikhaddah** (المخَدَّة) meaning the same. But in Portuguese, it is with an *f*. The

Portuguese *almofada* means a cushion.

Here is another example. It is the Arabic word **al-khuzāmā** (الْخُزَامَى) meaning lavender. It is *alhucema* in Spanish, but *alfazema* in Portuguese.

Eric: Very interesting indeed.

Ahmad: More interesting is the following example where both the *h* and *f* versions are Spanish. The Arabic word for basil is **al-ḥabaq** (الْحَبَق). This has assumed three forms in Spanish. They are:

- *alfábega*. In this word *h* has changed to *f*.
- *albahaca*. Here the Arabic *ḥ* has changed slightly, and has become *h*, but it has been shunted to the second place, for it should have been *alhabaca*.
- *alabega*. Here the *h* has been dropped.

In Portuguese, it is with an *f*, but the *b* has changed to *v*. It is *alfavaca*.

Eric: How many Arabic words there are in Spanish and Portuguese!

Ahmad: A lot! We have so far discussed only words which have the letter *kh*. Here are some more. The Arabic for lettuce is **al-khass** (الْخَسّ). It is *alface* in Portuguese. The Portuguese say, *fresco como uma alface.* It is equivalent to the English expression *as fresh as a daisy.* Its diminutive, *alfacinha*, is a playful nickname of the people of Lisbon so named because of their fondness for lettuce.

Eric: Have you finished with the *kh*-sound?

Ahmad: One last word. It is the Arabic **al-khanjar** (الْخَنْجَر) meaning a dagger or a scimitar. In both Spanish and Portuguese, it has become *alfanje*. As you can see, the letter *r* at the end of the word has been lost. This word has passed into some other European languages without the article **al-**. It is *khanjari* (χαντζαρι) in modern Greek, and *kinžal* (кинжал) in Russian.

Eric: So far we have seen the Arabic *h* and *kh* becoming *f* in Spanish and Portuguese. I would like to know what happens to the original Arabic *f*. Does it remain *f*?

Ahmad: Yes, of course, it remains unchanged. Here is an example. The Arabic **fulān** (فلان) meaning so-and-so became *fulano* in Spanish. Its feminine form is *fulana* which is exactly like the Arabic *fulānah*. The expression *fulano, zutano, mengano* means Tom, Dick and Harry. The diminutive *fulanito* means a little master.

Portuguese also has the same form, *fulano*, with the feminine *fulana*. It also has a shortened form, *fuão* in which the letter *l* has been lost, and the letter *n* is represented by the nasalisation of *ā.* Its feminine form is *fuā.*

Here are some more examples. The Arabic al-faqqūs (الفَقُّوس) or al-faqqūṣ (الفَقُّوص), meaning cucumber, is *alficoz* in Spanish.

The Portuguese *alferça, alferce* for a pick-axe is a corruption of the Arabic al-fa's (الفَأس) meaning axe or hatchet. An unwarranted *r* has crept in somehow.

Eric: This *r* is not unwarranted.

Ahmad: What is it then?

Eric: Remember you said both Spanish and Portuguese left out the *r* from *al-khanjar,* and turned the word into *alfanje*?

Ahmad: I did. Was I wrong?

Eric: No, no, you weren't. But I just wanted to suggest that the *r* in *alferça* is a compensation for the *r* lost in *alfanje.*

Ahmad: Well said!

Eric: Ahmad, the word *khanjar* that you mentioned earlier reminds me of another word. I read in a book sometime ago that *assassinate* is an Arabic word. What do you say to that?

Ahmad: I am very glad you asked me this question. I was in two minds about mentioning this word. Now that you have asked me about it, I'll tell you.

This word is believed to be Arabic, and this is

recorded in all etymological dictionaries. You know the word *hashish* which is now a drug made from the resin of the hemp plant. It is an Arabic word and means the Indian hemp. A hashish smoker is *ḥaššāš* in Arabic. Its plural is *ḥaššāšūn*, and in the oblique case, *ḥaššāšīn* (حَشَّاشِين). This is said to be the source of the word *assassin* meaning one who kills an important person for political reasons. Now, historically this word refers to the Nizārī Ismāʿīlī sect dating from the 11th to the 13th century known for murdering its enemies as a religious duty.

Eric: But why were they called *ḥaššāšīn*? Were they drug addicts?

Ahmad: That is a very pertinent question. It is said that members of this sect smoked hashish to induce ecstatic visions of paradise before setting out to undertake their murderous tasks. It is also said that the sect had created a simulation of the gardens of paradise into which the drugged commandos were introduced to have a foretaste of the pleasures of paradise.

Eric: And you think that these accounts are not true?

Ahmad: There are problems with this story. Two basic elements of the story need to be historically proved. These are:

a) that the members of this sect used hashish to help them carry out the murders,

b) that this sect was called *ḥaṧṧāṧīn* or *ḥaṧīṧī*s. But the fact is that there is no historical evidence to support either of these assumptions. Encyclopedia Britannica says, 'The historical evidence of this practice [of smoking hashish], however, is doubtful. The stories that were told by Marco Polo and other travellers about the gardens of paradise into which the drugged devotees were introduced to receive a foretaste of eternal bliss are not confirmed by any Isma'īlī source'.

And Encyclopedia of Islam (2nd edition) is also of the same opinion. It says, '...the use of drug by the sectaries, with or without secret gardens, is attested neither by Ismāʿīlī nor by serious Sunnī authors. Even the name *ḥaṧīṧiyya* is local to Syria and probably abusive. It was never used by contemporaries of the Persian or any other non-Syrian Ismāʿīlīs; even in Syria it was not used by the Isma'īlīs themselves'.

Eric: These are serious problems.

Ahmad: Yes, and that is why I did not want to mention this word.

Eric: Ahmad, we had better finish our discussion today. I have received a cable, and I must leave tomorrow.

Ahmad: You have received a cable.

Eric: You seem to have spotted an Arabic word there.

Ahmad: Yes, I sure have. It is *cable*.

Eric: The original meaning of *cable* is a strong rope.

Ahmad: And that's exactly what the Arabic ḥabl (حَبْل) means.

Eric: Do the linguists trace it to this Arabic word?

Ahmad: Yes. *OED* traces it as far as the Latin *capulum* meaning a halter and *Oxford Concise Dictionary of English Etymology* traces it further to the Arabic *ḥabl*.

Eric: I must take leave of you now, but we shall meet again soon.

Ahmad: *in šāʾ Allāh.*

Eric: Yes, of course, *in šāʾ Allāh*, or *oxalá!* I thank you very much for the very useful and interesting information about so many Arabic words that have permeated English and the other European languages. Some of them are key words like *zero, alkali, alcohol, benzene, coffee, magazine, cotton, average, tariff,* etc.

Ahmad: You can have an entire sentence made up of Arabic words like *'Check the sugar in your coffee, Admiral'.*

Eric: These words are so many and so important that one may almost say that we in Europe speak Arabic... Thank you once again, Ahmad.
Ahmad: Thank you too, Eric. Goodbye!

ርং ৪০

APPENDIX
NOTES ON STAR NAMES
MENTIONED IN CHAPTER 3

I have mentioned in Chapter 3 (p. 14) fifteen star names of Arabic origin, but as the tenor of the dialogue did not allow for their explanation at that time, I thought it would be useful to give the Arabic sources of these strange words in an appendix. For those interested in astronomy, I have added the astronomical names of these stars. Readers desirous of further information may consult the following books:

1) *Short Guide To Modern Star Names And Their Derivations* by Paul Kunitzsch and Tim Smart, Otto Harrassowitz, Wiesbaden, 1986.

2) *Untersuchungen zur Sternnomenklatur der Araber* by Paul Kunitzsch, Otto Harrassowitz, Wiesbaden, 1961.

3) *Arabische Sternnamen in Europa* by Paul Kunitzsch, Otto Harrassowitz, Wiesbaden, 1959.

4) *Der Almagest* by Paul Kunitzsch, Otto Harrassowitz, Wiesbaden, 1974.

184 APPENDIX

5) *Star Names, Their Lore And Meaning* by Richard Hinckley Allen, Dover Publications, Inc., New York, 1963.

Following are the star names and their derivations.

- *Achernar* (α Eridani) from the Arabic **ākhir al-nahr** (آخِرُ النَّهر), the River's End. Another form of this same Arabic word, *Acamar*, is applied to θ Eridani.
- *Alpheratz* (α Andromedae) from the Arabic **al-faras** (الفَرَس) the Horse. An alternate name of this star is *Sirrah* which is from the Arabic **surrah al-faras** (سُرّة الفَرَس), the Hores's Navel.
- *Azelfafage* (π¹ Cygni) from the Arabic **al-sulhafāh** (السُّلحفاة), the Tortoise.
- *Benetnasch* (η Ursae Maioris) from the Arabic **banāt naʿš** (بَنَاتُ نَعْش), the Pallbearers (literally, the Daughters of the Bier). An alternate name of this star is *Alkaid* which is from the Arabic **al-qāʾid** (القائِد), the Leader, i.e. Leader of the Pallbearers.
- *Denebola* (β Leonis) from the Arabic **dhanab al-asad** (ذنَبُ الأسَد), the Lion's Tail. Here the last three letters of the word *asad* have been omitted.

- *Dschubba* (δ Scorpionis) from the Arabic **jabhaħ al-ʿaqrab** (جَبْهَة العَقْرَب), the Scorpion's Forehead.
- *Fomalhaut* (α Piscis Austrini) from the Arabic **fam al-ḥūt** (فَمُ الحُوت), the Mouth of the Fish.
- *Menkalinan* (β Aurigae) from the Arabic **mankib dhī l-ʿinān** (مَنكِبُ ذي العِنـان), the Shoulder of the Reinholder.
- *Rasalgethi* (α Herculis) from the Arabic **ra's al-jāthī** (رأسُ الجاثى), the Kneeler's Head.
- *Sadalmelik* (α Aquarii) from the Arabic **saʿd al-malik** (سَعْدُ المَلِك), the Luck of the King applied to α and o Aquarii in Arabic astronomy.
- *Toliman* (α Centauri) from the Arabic **al-ẓulmān** (الظلمـان), the Ostriches. An alternate name of this star is *Rigil Kentaurus* which is from the Arabic **rijl qanṭūris** (رجْلُ قنطـورس), Centaur's Foot.
- *Unukalhai* (α Serpentis) from the Arabic **ʿunuq al-ḥayyaħ** (عُنـق الحَيَـة), the Serpent's Neck.
- *Wezen* (δ Canis Maioris) from the Arabic **al-wazn** (الوَزن), the Weight.
- *Zubenelgenubi* (α Librae) from the Arabic **al-zubānā al-janūbī** (الزُبـانى الجَنـوبي), the Southern Claw (of the Scorpion).

○ *Zubeneschamali* (β Librae) from the Arabic **al-zubānā al-šamālī** (الزبانى الشمالي), the Northern Claw (of the Scorpion).

INDEX OF ENGLISH WORDS

An *n* following a number signifies that the word occurs in the footnote.

INDEX OF ARABIC WORDS

In the arrangement of words, diacritical marks have been ignored.
An *n* following a number signifies that the word occurs in the footnote.